ARE THERE REALLY
MANSIONS
IN
HEAVEN?

ARE THERE REALLY
MANSIONS
IN
HEAVEN?

It's a family affair

SECOND EDITION

CLEMENT C. BUTLER

RESOURCE *Publications* · Eugene, Oregon

ARE THERE *REALLY* MANSIONS IN HEAVEN?

Resource Publications
An Imprint of Wipf and Stock Publishers
199 W. 8th Ave., Suite 3
Eugene, OR 97401

www.wipfandstock.com
PAPERBACK ISBN: 978-1-6667-1757-0
HARDCOVER ISBN: 978-1-6667-1758-7
EBOOK ISBN: 978-1-6667-1759-4

Unless otherwise indicated, Scripture references are taken from the King James

Version of the Bible. Please send comments and questions to

approvedworkmanministries@yahoo.com

Please visit our website: www.approvedworkmanministries.com

Follow us on Twitter @242teacher

CONTENTS

CONTENDERS FOR THE FAITH

INTRODUCTION

Why does an author phrase a book title as a question? More often than not, the intention is to present a thought-provoking, engaging topic. However, if we already have resolute convictions about the subject matter, sometimes, we look at the book with diminished interest. On the other hand, if we are uncertain and have unanswered questions related to the topic, we are intrigued to pursue the perspectives being offered. Hopefully, as it pertains to this book, the latter disposition prevails.

Throughout our lives, we listen to opinions and discussions on certain topics and adopt some of the principles as truth without really verifying the information for ourselves. Similarly, in the promotion of church doctrine, leaders sometimes create ideologies that are simply designed to appeal to human emotions. Unfortunately, some of these precepts cannot be substantiated by Scripture. One such tenet is the popular teaching regarding mansions in heaven.

Over the years, I have seen several pictures of majestic homes in a "heavenly environment," which are purported to resemble mansions in heaven. Howbeit, these images are based solely on human imaginations and promoted by those whom we consider authorities when it comes to spiritual things. As a standard, we have many examples in Scripture regarding how we ought to measure all teachings. For instance, despite receiving the Word of God with all readiness of mind, the believers in Berea searched the Scriptures daily to determine if the things they heard were so (Acts 17:11). They recognized the tremendous value in studying the Word to validate doctrine. Furthermore, for a doctrine to have a firm foundation, it cannot be based on one scripture, but rather on the reconciliation of all scriptures regarding a particular subject matter.

Are there really mansions in heaven? Based on a precise examination of Scripture, in conjunction with implementing the principles of rightly dividing the Word of God, I submit that the answer is no! However, in accordance with that response, another question presents itself. If the mansions Jesus promised are not consistent with traditional thinking, what message was He actually conveying?

In answering that question, this book first establishes a foundation by providing principles for a better understanding of the Scriptures. This is followed by a general context of the Gospels in order to understand their prevailing messages. Based on this premise, significant attention is placed on the Gospel of John and its overall context to better understand John Chapter 14. In this regard, important terms such as "the Father's house," "mansions," and "I go to prepare a place for you" are discussed in detail. Finally, the book addresses the subject of eternal inheritance and where believers will spend eternity.

To be clear, this book does not negate the sureness of eternal life or our eternal inheritance of the kingdom of God, but specifically, whether or not there are actually mansions in heaven. In accordance with tradition and common teaching, I know this conclusion may not be popular. However, after reading this book, I am certain your sentiments concerning mansions will be different.

It is my hope that as you read this book, you will fully understand the true context in which Jesus was speaking and the fundamental principle He was addressing. May you receive a greater appreciation for the truth of Scripture, God's purpose for us, and the significance of being members of His family.

CHAPTER ONE

Foundational Principles

THE HOPE OF A HOME

What is it about a house that intrigues us? Outside the realm of a status symbol, a house at its core represents a sanctuary, security, and a place of rest. It is the dream many of us strive for.

On a more intrinsic level, it provides a sense of belonging and achievement. I remember the overwhelming feeling of accomplishment I had when I moved into my first home. I finally had a place of my own. Perhaps this is why the promise of mansions in heaven is enthusiastically embraced by many believers. Certainly, from an eternal perspective, this "promise" seems to imply some of the same sentiments we attach to an earthly home.

As a kid, I recall my mom taking my siblings and me on Sunday afternoon drives through what I considered upscale neighborhoods. To take it all in, we drove slowly, and I was always fascinated by the size, design, and beauty of the homes. On one of these occasions, while reflecting on the fact that we lived in a small apartment at that time, I turned and said to my mom, "When I get older, I'm going to buy you a house." With sheer gratitude in her eyes, she looked at me and replied, "thank you."

My mother was a hardworking woman but despite her tremendous efforts, I realized the dream of homeownership was evading her. Naïve and feeling a sense of obligation, I figured it was the least I could do. Unfortunately, she passed away before I could make good on my promise but occasionally, I still reflect on the commitment I made to her and how it made her feel.

For many people, the most expensive, single material investment they will make during their lives is the acquisition of a home. In most cases, it requires tremendous sacrifice, so the joy of achieving it is enormous. However, even for those who experience the thrill of homeownership, they still desire what is considered a "dream home." It is the one that we envision before the realities of our financial restraints cause us to settle for more modest accommodations.

While we can agree that the physical building does not provide the "homely feeling," and the essence of family surpasses the actual structure, the concept of a mansion still intrigues us. In that vein, for the better portion of my life, the idea of mansions in heaven was a non-negotiable fact. When I compared my present dwelling to what was supposedly "prepared for me," there was a tremendous feeling of anticipation. Furthermore, John 14:2, along with the anecdotes and songs associated with mansions left no doubt in my mind there was one reserved in heaven for me. I especially liked the song, "Mansion over the Hilltop." In fact, every time

I heard that song, I would get goosebumps and envision my home in the sky.

MANSIONS OVER THE HILLTOP

I'm satisfied with just a cottage below
A little silver and a little gold
But in that city where the ransomed will shine
I want a gold one that's silver lined
I've got a mansion just over the hilltop
In that bright land where we'll never grow old
And some day yonder we will never more wander
But walk on streets that are purest gold
Don't think me poor or deserted or lonely
I'm not discouraged I'm heaven bound
I'm but a pilgrim in search of the city
I want a mansion, a harp and a crown
Written by Ira Stanphil

Many of us live in economic environments that limit our ability to buy what we ideally want. Therefore, we are forced to make concessions and adopt the position of contentment, particularly, in relation to the size and amenities of our houses. Consequently, as it pertains to the topic of mansions in heaven, the response is often, "I may not get what I want down here, but in heaven, there's a mansion reserved for me." Hence, the concept of owning a mansion in heaven has become the ultimate reward and entitlement due to the ordeals and sacrifices experienced on Earth.

In harmony with the concept of being a stranger or pilgrim on Earth, the idea of a permanent dwelling in heaven engenders tremendous hope in believers. In addition, the words of the song suggest that if we defer or are denied extravagant accommodations on the earth, elaborate mansions are preserved for us in heaven. Hence, we make sacrifices with the expectation that what is promised supersedes what is forfeited on Earth. While the premise of this has merit, the question remains, is the promise of mansions based on John 14:2 included in this concept?

THE PROMISE FOR THIS PRESENT TIME AND THE TIME TO COME

What does Scripture say is the recompense for denying ourselves the material and emotional attachments of this life and following Christ? Jesus provides some insight in Luke Chapter 18 that will answer this question:

18. And a certain ruler asked him, saying, Good Master, what shall I do to inherit eternal life?
19. And Jesus said unto him, Why callest thou me good? none is good, save one, that is, God.
20. Thou knowest the commandments, Do not commit adultery, Do not kill, Do not steal, Do not bear false witness, Honour thy father and thy mother.
21. And he said, All these have I kept from my youth up.

22. Now when Jesus heard these things, he said unto him, Yet lackest thou one thing: sell all that thou hast, and distribute unto the poor, and thou shalt have treasure in heaven: and come, follow me.

23. And when he heard this, he was very sorrowful: for he was very rich.

24. And when Jesus saw that he was very sorrowful, he said, How hardly shall they that have riches enter into the kingdom of God!

25. For it is easier for a camel to go through a needle's eye, than for a rich man to enter into the kingdom of God.

26. And they that heard it said, Who then can be saved?

27. And he said, The things which are impossible with men are possible with God.

28. Then Peter said, Lo, we have left all, and followed thee.

29. And he said unto them, Verily I say unto you, There is no man that hath left house, or parents, or brethren, or wife, or children, for the kingdom of God's sake,

30. Who shall not receive manifold more in this present time, and in the world to come life everlasting. (Luke 18:18-30)

In this passage, we are presented with two scenarios in relation to the reward for material and emotional renouncement and following Christ. One pertains to the benefits of this life and the other applies to the world to come.

While in conversation with a certain rich man, Jesus admonished him to give his possessions to the poor and follow Him that he might have treasure in heaven. To be specific, He is saying, "Give up your source of dependency and instead, place your trust in me." Jesus used the term "treasure in heaven" to essentially create a contrast with "treasure on Earth." As the man had great possessions, the statement targeted valuing earthly riches above that which is heavenly. In reality, this expression was based on the principle of Matthew 6:21, which says, "Where your treasure is, there will your heart be also." Hence, Jesus was advocating a change in the condition of the heart where the material things of this world have a diminished value compared to that which is heavenly or spiritual.

Consequently, based on the rich man's refusal, Jesus said to His disciples that it was easier for a camel to go through the eye of a needle than for a rich man to enter the kingdom of God. In this illustration, the rich man placed greater emphasis on his earthy possessions than on spiritual values. Upon hearing this exchange, Peter said to Jesus that they had left all and followed Him. In other words, "We have already done what you required of the rich man. Therefore, what benefits are in store for us?" In response, Jesus said that based on the deferment of possessions and letting go of close relations for the kingdom's sake, you shall receive much more in this present time, and in the world to come, you shall receive everlasting life. Let's look at these two scenarios.

THE PRESENT TIME

The word "time" in Luke 18:30 is the Greek word *kairos,* which means a limited period of time or a fixed or definite time. Therefore, the reference to "present time" in the verse speaks of *the present age in which we exist or this life.* Hence, Jesus is saying that when we forfeit what we have or when we exchange "earthly treasure" for "heavenly treasure," we have the promise of earthly blessing in greater proportion than what we originally possessed. That promise is for this life. With that said, having "treasure in heaven" does not infer that we won't have material blessings; instead, it simply means that our hearts are not consumed with them. Much more can be bestowed in this present time because if required, even that can be given away willingly and without hesitation. Not being attached to material things allows us to easily walk away from them.

In harmony with this concept, Jesus provided the parable of "The Pearl of Great Price" in Matthew 13:45-46. The core message of this parable is that we have to be willing to divest ourselves of everything we possess once we find that which is of greater value, in this instance, the kingdom of God.

45. Again, the kingdom of heaven is like unto a merchant man, seeking goodly pearls:
46. Who, when he had found one pearl of great price, went and sold all that he had, and bought it. (Matthew 13:45-46)

I reiterate that in accordance with Luke Chapter 18, when we renounce our earthly attachments for the kingdom's sake, the promise of much more is not exclusively reserved for our eternal existence, but it is also for this present time. This is the same principle Jesus offers in Matthew 6:33, which says that if we seek first the kingdom of God and His righteousness *all the things we need will be added unto us* (in this life). Therefore, based on the conclusions offered in Luke Chapter 18, it should be apparent that there is no correlation between the concept of "mansions in heaven" as a result of settling for "a cottage" on Earth as the song signifies.

THE WORLD TO COME

In addition to the promise of receiving much more in this present time, Luke 18:30 also says that in the world to come, you shall receive eternal life. In this instance, the word "world" is the Greek word *aion,* which means an age, a period of time, or eternity. This statement is associated with the fact that the gift of God is eternal life (John 3:16). Hence, there is a dual reward for forfeiting our earthly attachments. One pertains to this time and the other refers to the world to come. However, an important question is where will the promise of eternal life be enjoyed? Will it be in heaven or on Earth? As the intent of this chapter is to first provide a good foundation for this discussion, the answer to this question will be addressed in Chapter 6.

A MORE SURE WORD: WHAT IS SEEN/ HEARD VERSUS WHAT IS WRITTEN

In most cases, the condition of sound doctrine is that it requires more than one witness of Scripture to confirm its veracity. In fact, according to the Bible, for a word to be established, two or three witnesses are required (Matthew 18:16, 2 Corinthians 13:1). Additionally, doctrine should be based on the reconciliation of the "whole of Scripture." However, many of the conclusions we have made concerning mansions in heaven are derived from a solitary reference: John 14:1-3 where Jesus says:

1. Let not your heart be troubled: ye believe in God, believe also in me.
2. *In my Father's house are many mansions: if it were not so, I would have told you. I go to prepare a place for you.*
3. And if I go and prepare a place for you, I will come again, and receive you unto myself; that where I am, there ye may be also.

What precisely is Jesus referring to in this passage? Is He really talking about actual mansions? Based on popular belief, did He truly leave Earth to start a building project in heaven? Is there another verse of Scripture that can be used to support the position of heavenly mansions?

Without another witness of Scripture, the illustrations of mansions in heaven are based on the accounts provided by various individuals. Consequently, over the years, there have been numerous stories and movies based on the reports of those who have purportedly seen mansions in heaven. However, always remember that the written Word of God is the final authority on all subject matters. Therefore, as a principle, we should always measure everything that is said by the *objective standard* of the Word of God. In this regard, doctrine should not be based on subjective reasoning or opinions but rather, on the objective standard of Scripture.

As a tenet of rightly dividing the Word of God, *what is written always has greater value than what we see or hear.* Too often, we seem to place equal or greater emphasis on what we personally see or hear than on the Word of God. However, in 2 Peter 1:16-21, Peter offers a comparison that distinguishes between what is seen or heard versus the written Word of God.

16. For we have not followed cunningly devised fables, when we made known unto you the power and coming of our Lord Jesus Christ, but were eyewitnesses of his majesty.

17. For he received from God the Father honour and glory, when there came such a voice to him from the excellent glory, This is my beloved Son, in whom I am well pleased.

18. And this voice which came from heaven we heard, when we were with him in the holy mount.

19. We have also a more sure word of prophecy; whereunto ye do well that ye take heed, as unto a light that shineth in a dark place, until the day dawn, and the day star arise in your hearts:

20. Knowing this first, that no prophecy of the scripture is of any private interpretation.

21. For the prophecy came not in old time by the will of man: but holy men of God spake as they were moved by the Holy Ghost. (2 Peter 1:16-21)

To convey the authenticity of the gospel of Christ, Peter says their teachings were not based on imaginary stories or elaborate fairy tales. They were not fictitious accounts like the stories of "Snow White" or "Cinderella." Rather, they were actually eyewitnesses of Christ's majesty. In other words, Peter is saying they could validate what they were preaching and who Christ is because they saw Him for themselves. Peter substantiates this by referring to Christ's transfiguration recorded in Matthew Chapter 17. While Peter was in the mountain with Jesus, James, and John, Christ was transfigured. Let us take a look at the account:

1. And after six days Jesus taketh Peter, James, and John his brother, and bringeth them up into an high mountain apart,

2. And was transfigured before them: and his face did shine as the sun, and his raiment was white as the light.

3. And, behold, there appeared unto them Moses and Elias talking with him.

4. Then answered Peter, and said unto Jesus, Lord, it is good for us to be here: if thou wilt, let us make here three tabernacles; one for thee, and one for Moses, and one for Elias.

5. While he yet spake, behold, a bright cloud over-
shadowed them: and behold a voice out of the
cloud, which said, This is my beloved Son, in
whom I am well pleased; hear ye him. (Matthew
17:1-5)

In rehearsing the event, Peter says while they were with
Jesus on the holy mountain, they *saw* and *heard* something.
Consequently, based on what transpired, they were able to
provide an eyewitness account of what they saw and heard.
They saw Christ transfigured to the point that His face shone
as the sun, and His raiment was as white as the light. They
saw Christ in His glory and majesty. Furthermore, Moses and
Elijah also appeared and spoke with Christ concerning His
death (Luke 9:31).

Captivated by the encounter, Peter offered to build three
tabernacles: one for Christ, one for Moses, and one for Elijah.
However, in order to correct Peter, as well as validate Jesus'
position, the Father then spoke. He said, "This is my beloved
Son in whom I am well pleased; hear ye Him." What was the
purpose of God saying this? Peter's statement suggested that
Christ, Moses, and Elijah were on equal footing. Therefore,
Peter wanted to erect three shrines to commemorate the
occasion. However, the appearance of Moses and Elijah with
Christ symbolized something more significant.

Moses served as the embodiment of the law (2 Corinthians
3:15) and Elijah depicted the prophets (Matthew 5:17-20).
Therefore, in unison, they both illustrated the old covenant
in its entirety (Luke 16:16). What is interesting is that Peter
made the statement concerning building the tabernacles as

Moses and Elijah were departing (Luke 9:33). While Peter wanted to hold onto the former, God was transitioning to something new. Hence, this event not only portrayed Christ as the One to fulfill the law and the prophets, but it also served as a transitioning from the old covenant to the new covenant. Moreover, with the Father specifically identifying Jesus as "His Son," this created a clear distinction between Christ, Moses, and Elijah. In addition, the Father's admonition to, "Hear ye Him," was designed to draw attention from Moses and Elijah and place it exclusively on Christ as the sole communicator of the Father's purpose. This exact sentiment is also expressed in Hebrews Chapter 1:

1. God who at sundry times and in divers manners spake in time past unto the fathers by the prophets,
2. Hath in these last days spoken unto us by His Son, whom He hath appointed heir of all thing, by home also He made the worlds. (Hebrews 1:1-2)

In essence, this entire experience on the mountain served as the passing of the baton from the law and the prophets to Jesus Christ, as the agent through whom the Father speaks.

In summarizing the event and staying on topic, Peter is saying that what they saw and heard allowed them to speak from an eyewitness perspective. In particular, what they heard represented *a sure word of prophecy*. They could say without a doubt, "God spoke to us!" However, in making a comparison, he says in 2 Peter 1:19, "*We have also a more sure word of prophecy.*" On one hand, we have the account of what was gathered by means of sensory perception and that was authentic. On the other hand, we have something that is even more reliable than that. What is more reliable than what you see and hear? Peter points out that what is written offers more stability and steadfastness than what our senses perceive. Certainly, what we gather with our senses has credibility, but the written Word of God outweighs the determinations of our senses. This is because sometimes our senses can be manipulated by our own desires or what we have been exposed to.

Oftentimes, people say, "God said this or that or I have seen this or that." While this may be a sure word, there is, indeed, something more reliable. What is written is more steadfast because every other narrative or conclusion has to be in harmony with the written Word of God. It is the barometer by which everything that is said or done is measured. In addition, the written Word is the more sure word of prophecy because holy men spoke as they were inspired by the Holy Ghost.

2 Timothy 3:16 says, "All Scripture is given by inspiration of God," which means it is "God-breathed." Therefore, by the illustration offered in 2 Peter 1:16-21, the principle is that the written Word of God holds precedence above what is seen and heard. It is the objective standard that is not reliant on subjective reasoning or human analysis. We cannot place greater value on these reports above what is written in Scripture. A point of reference is Matthew Chapter 4 when Jesus was being tempted by the Devil. His response of "It is written" was the recurring theme, which signifies the strength and sureness of the written Word of God.

In connecting this principle to this discussion, do we hold the reports of those who have purportedly seen mansions in heaven above the account of the written Word of God? Do we conclude that what others have supposedly seen or heard is equal to or greater than what is written? Like Peter, let us determine that we have a more sure word of prophecy and that Scripture is the highest authority on all subjects.

THE BENEFITS OF TRUTH

As I often advocate in my writings, one of the benefits of truth is that it neither deprives nor leaves you in a lesser state. Sometimes, even in relation to doctrine, we are afraid to let go of what we have relied on because we feel the alternative is of less value. Additionally, another benefit of truth is that it out values what it replaces—the things you previously enjoyed or experienced. Therefore, truth brings with it enrichment and does not diminish.

On one occasion, while discussing the topic of mansions in heaven with a friend, there was still a bit of disallowance regarding the subject despite his acceptance of the truth of Scripture. The justification for his position was that the idea of no mansions in heaven would adversely impact one of the long-held doctrines of the church and deflate the hope of many believers. However, if hope is based on a misunderstanding or misinterpretation of Scripture, it's really a false expectation. In reality, with such false hope, we do a greater disservice to the people of God.

As a consequence of truth, it is not the intent of this book to simply take away the traditional concept of mansions in heaven with no meaningful replacement. Rather, its purpose is to offer the true perspective of the topic to provide enrichment and enlightenment of the Father's purpose. This then fosters a genuine hope that is steadfast and unshakable.

CONTEXT AND PERSPECTIVE OF SCRIPTURE

How many times have you said something that was misconstrued or misinterpreted? For many of us, this is prevalent in the work environment, at home, and even in relationships. How do you respond? The common response tends to be, "That is not what I meant," or "You took what I said out of context." When this occurs, the original message of the communicator is changed and made to fit the perspective of the receiver. Regrettably, many of us frequently take Scripture out of context which alters the original message.

As a principle, having the correct perspective of Scripture requires having the correct context of Scripture. Therefore, our perspectives on specific topics are incorrect because our context regarding the subject is flawed. Hence, an accurate perspective on mansions in heaven can only be obtained when a proper context of Scripture is first established. Therefore, *proper context results in proper perspective.*

CONTEXT OF SCRIPTURE

According to *Literary Devices*, "Context is the background, environment, setting, framework, or surroundings of events or occurrences. Simply, context means circumstances forming a background of an event, idea, or statement, in such a way as to enable readers to understand the narrative or a literary piece." Anytime something is said, for there to be clarity, the context must be known.

Similar to the above definition, context, as it pertains to Scripture, means the following:

- The inter-related conditions in which Scripture exists or occurs.
- The circumstances or setting in which an event in Scripture occurs.
- The part of a text or statement (passage) that surrounds a particular word or verse and determines its meaning.
- The verse of Scripture that precedes and follows another verse or passage and contributes to its full meaning or influences its meaning or effect.
- The set of circumstances or facts that surround a particular verse, passage, book, or testament.

Based on the definition of "context," when reading or studying the Scriptures, it is essential to take into consideration, not only the verse being studied but also the environment in which the verse exists. By following this principle, the verse or passage is not viewed independently but is interpreted in consideration of surrounding events. Hence, attention has to be given to the circumstances in which the verse occurs. Furthermore, what was said prior to the verse, as well as what is yet to be said, has to be taken into account. When verses of Scripture are used separately to stand alone and independent of the context, this results in fragments of the context and an incorrect perspective. Within the scope of the context of Scripture, there are four constituents that must be applied for there to be a correct understanding of Scripture.

PRINCIPLES FOR THE CONTEXT OF SCRIPTURE

- **The Passage Context:** Verses of a particular chapter must not be interpreted in isolation from the chapter, passage, or book under consideration. A passage context includes all the verses and chapters of a particular book, which focus on a specific subject.
- **The Book Context:** Each book of the Bible has a central theme running through its chapters. The context of the verse has to be considered within the context of the entire book in which it is found.
- **The Testament Context:** Each Testament of the Bible has a general context. The general theme of the Old Testament is the law and the general theme of the New Testament is grace. Therefore, the verse being considered has to be examined in the context of the Testament in which it exists.

- **The Volume of the Book or Whole of Scripture Context:** To get the context on a particular subject, all scriptures pertaining to the topic have to be examined.

As we advance in our discussion on mansions in heaven, these principles will serve as fundamental components. Once the context of a verse, passage, or book regarding a particular subject has been established, then a proper perspective can be achieved.

PERSPECTIVE OF SCRIPTURE

In plain language, perspective simply means the particular way we look at or think about something. Perspective as it pertains to Scripture means:

- To see the Scriptures as God intends for them to be seen or from His point of view
- To ensure that all passages of Scripture used are in true relationship with the whole of Scripture
- The capacity to view Scripture in its true relation or relative importance
- To see the Scriptures in their true relationship

In harmony with the definition of "perspective," it should be evident that to have the proper perspective of Scripture, it is important to examine the relationship scriptures share with each other. Too many times, entire doctrines are built from a single verse or an incorrect perspective of that verse. Therefore, the discussion of mansions in heaven will be studied within the scope of the principles of the context of Scripture and the perspective of Scripture.

The intent of this chapter is to create a good foundation for the discussion on mansions in heaven. Rather than diving headfirst into the topic, the strategy is to establish meaningful principles for a better context on the topic. Let us revisit these concepts:

- We concluded that renouncing material and emotional attachments brings reward in this present time, as well as the world to come.
- Based on the example of Scripture, what is written is more reliable than what is seen or heard.
- The benefit truth brings is that it provides enlightenment and enrichment.
- Once we have the proper context of Scripture, this results in the proper perspective of Scripture.

CHAPTER TWO

The Context of the Gospels

GETTING TO THE POINT

Among my colleagues, I have developed a reputation for asking stirring questions to spark conversations on particular subjects. However, even though I ask the questions, I am sometimes also pressed to provide the responses. In truth, I often use these forums as an opportunity to solicit feedback on various subjects about the books I write. With that said, on one occasion, I asked them, "Are there really mansions in heaven?" After hearing several responses, I was asked to provide my perspective. However, during my delivery, either out of impatience or sheer eagerness, I was admonished by my colleagues to simply get to the point. However, considering the interest they exhibited, I am inclined to think it was the latter of the two. Nevertheless, when it comes to receiving information, there seems to be an increased tendency toward short answers rather than to endure lengthy explanations. Certainly, in some instances, this is warranted, while in others, it is not.

To achieve the designation of a Competent Communicator, the Toastmasters program has a ten-speech project. The title of phase three is, "Get to the Point." The objective of that monologue is to clearly state the goal of the speech and ensure every element of your address focuses on that goal. It requires organizing your speech with a general and specific purpose and arranging it to achieve that aim.

Being a Toastmaster of Club 8720, I certainly understand the importance of getting to the point. However, "getting to the point" is not intended to simply provide an abbreviated response but rather, one that accomplishes the designed purpose. Its objective is not to eliminate necessary information but to ensure that what is being offered is relevant to the discussion. With that said, for a topic that is so entrenched in Christian doctrine, a systematic approach to correct such teaching is necessary. Therefore, in addressing this subject, getting to the point involves a lengthy, yet, focused discussion.

If I simply offered the conclusion that there were no mansions in heaven and supported this position with a couple of scriptures, would that be a persuasive argument? Certainly, some consider heavenly mansions to be a pillar of church doctrine; therefore, information that negates this has to be substantial. With that said, a comprehensive response produces wholeness regarding topics of this nature. At the same time, it gives us the ability to properly explain our positions to others without fear of contradiction.

Moreover, whenever we hear a teaching, we have to be disciplined enough to search the Scriptures to determine if the doctrine is based on truth (Acts 17:11). However, oftentimes we readily accept teaching based on how it makes us feel or who said it. Nevertheless, we are admonished in 2 Timothy 2:15 to "Study to show thyself approved unto God, a workman that needeth not to be ashamed, rightly dividing the word of truth." Study, regardless of the discipline, requires time, effort, and careful examination of material relative to the subject matter.

THE GOSPELS AND THE MESSAGE OF THE KINGDOM

The Gospel of John represents one of the four Gospels, which details the life and purpose of Jesus Christ. In unison, they all have a singular announcement, which is the message of the kingdom of God or the kingdom of heaven. As a matter of principle, it should be noted that both these terms refer to the same thing and are used interchangeably in the Gospels in identical discussions. For example:

- Matthew 5:3 and Luke 6:20
- Matthew 11:11 and Luke 7:28

First, the expression "kingdom of God" is an acknowledgment that Yahweh, as God, has a kingdom. As a King, it ascribes kingdom ownership or dominion to Him. In support of this, the phrase "kingdom of heaven" identifies the extent or range of the kingdom over which God rules. Furthermore, the term also creates a distinction between the kingdoms of the earth and God's heavenly kingdom.

In summary, one term conveys who the government belongs to, while the other explains the extent or range of His dominion. Therefore, in promoting His agenda, when Jesus officially started His ministry, the very first thing He said in Matthew 4:17 was, "Repent, for the kingdom of heaven is at hand." After establishing His platform of the kingdom, everything that He said and did in the Gospels was to promote this agenda.

After making His declaration regarding the kingdom of heaven, Jesus then had to explain what the kingdom is or its characteristics. For example, during the initial chapters of the Gospel of Matthew, Jesus spoke of entering the kingdom of heaven, inheriting the kingdom of heaven, and seeking first the kingdom of heaven. However, up to this point, He had offered no precise explanation of what the kingdom of heaven is. In a general sense, the audience understood what a kingdom entailed, but specifically, there was no understanding of the characteristics of God's kingdom. This is why by use of comparison, He began by contrasting the ideals of religion to the attributes of the kingdom of God.

Often, to accentuate the qualities of a higher standard, it is compared to what used to be the accepted norm. To accomplish this, Matthew Chapter 5 is saturated with the phrase, "You have heard" or "It hath been said," followed by the alternative expression, "But I say unto you." In essence, Jesus was introducing a new way of thinking or a kingdom culture that was in opposition to religious principles.

As it pertains to the particular manner of conveying the message of the kingdom, the Gospels of Matthew, Mark, and Luke have distinct perspectives when compared to that of the

Gospel of John. In fact, the first three Gospels are generally labeled as the "Synoptic Gospels," which simply means they all share a similar or common view.

When we fully examine the content of these three Gospels: Matthew, Mark, Luke, it becomes apparent that they focus more on the nature of the kingdom of heaven or what it is like. To this end, they use many parables to express the message of the kingdom.

THE USE OF PARABLES TO EXPLAIN THE KINGDOM

Jesus stated that the primary reason for parables was to present the mysteries of the kingdom of heaven but with obscurity or in a hidden manner.

> 10. And the disciples came, and said unto him, Why speakest thou unto them in parables?
> 11. He answered and said unto them, Because it is given unto you to know the mysteries of the kingdom of heaven, but to them it is not given. (Matthew 13:10-11)

Apart from its main purpose, the use of parables also satisfied the principle of Scripture that invisible or spiritual things are understood by nature or by the things that are made (Romans 1:20). As the fundamentals of the kingdom of heaven were unknown to humanity, Jesus used identifiable things to illustrate them. A parable is a metaphor, which uses examples of everyday experiences or nature to explain the spiritual operations of the kingdom. It is only through the lens of a pure heart (good soil) that it becomes an identifiable language to produce change. Unless the heart is pure, it will be perceived as just a story and the true spiritual operation will be missed.

Particularly, in this modern time where the concept of democracy is more pervasive than that of a kingdom, the illustrations of Jesus offer tremendous kingdom insight. Based on historical accounts and movies, the image of a kingdom seems like a foreign entity and removed from the lives of ordinary people. Therefore, through parables, the principles of the kingdom became more identifiable and relatable. Notice that Jesus, in His use of the parables, used examples from a broad range of experiences: agriculture, relationships, baking, and fishing. Some of the parables (like the ones in the chart below) are prefaced with the phrase, "the kingdom of heaven is like," while others are not. Nevertheless, all the parables contain elements that describe the fundamentals of the kingdom.

The chart provides a depiction of the parables, which speak distinctly concerning the kingdom of heaven or the kingdom of God.

PARABLES ILLUSTRATING
THE KINGDOM OF GOD

Parable	Matthew	Mark	Luke
The Wheat and Tares	13:24-30 13:36-43		
The Mustard Seed	13:31-32	4:30-32	13:18-19
The Leaven	13:33		13:20
The Buried Treasure	13:44		
The Pearl	13:45-46		
The Net	13:47-50		
The Growth of the Seed		4:26-29	
The Unforgiving Servant	18:21-35		
The Vineyard Workers	20:1-16		
The Banquet	22:1-14		
The Ten Virgins	25:1-13		
The Talents	25:14-30		

THE GOSPEL OF JOHN

Unlike the other three gospels, John takes a different approach in communicating the message of the kingdom of God. Contrary to Matthew, Mark, and Luke, John contains no parables; yet, its kingdom concentration is the same. The focus of this Gospel is the relationship between the Father and the Son in a kingdom environment. Furthermore, the book also serves as a blueprint for our relationship with the Father as we are also His sons. Therefore, to appreciate how sons of the kingdom should operate, it is imperative to have a comprehensive understanding of the Gospel of John. *In essence, this Gospel is a book about the relationship between the Father and the Son.*

As discussed, Matthew, Mark, and Luke offer a comprehensive description of the *nature* of the Kingdom. Throughout these books, Jesus uses an abundance of parables to explain what the kingdom of heaven is. However, even though the Gospel of John also has the kingdom as a platform, its primary communication is the nature of the Son of the kingdom and His relationship with the Father. In addition, the first three Gospels focus more on what Jesus did, while John places greater emphasis on who Jesus is. In that vein, throughout the Gospel, Jesus is deliberate in conveying this message. For example, He says:

- I am the Bread of Life (John 6:35).
- I am the Light of the World (John 8:12).
- I am the Good Shepherd (John 10:11).
- I am the Resurrection and the Life (John 11:25).
- I am the Way, the Truth, and the Life (John 14:6).
- I am the True Vine (John 15:1).

What is interesting is that individually, and with a kingdom backdrop, each of the four Gospels portrays Christ from a different perspective. For instance, Matthew depicts Him as King. Mark describes Him as a servant. Luke portrays Him as the Son of Man, and John presents Him as the Son of God. Even though these illustrations are not totally exclusive to these books, they certainly represent the predominant message of each Gospel. In John's communication of Jesus as the Son of God, not only is he emphatic that Jesus is God, but that He also came in the capacity of a Son. Therefore, these two dynamics: He is God, and He came in the capacity of a Son become the recurring theme of the book.

Now that we have a general understanding of the context of the Gospels, which is a kingdom concept, let's look specifically at the Gospel of John in consideration of mansions in the Father's house.

CHAPTER THREE

The Context of the Gospel of John

CHANGING THE PERSPECTIVE

Even though John's Gospel differs from the other Gospels in a general sense, it is still consistent in its kingdom message. Hence, like the other three Gospels, the kingdom of God is pervasive throughout its chapters. Despite not containing parables to illustrate the kingdom, John approaches the subject from the position of Jesus as a Son of the kingdom. Therefore, with the focus of the book being the relationship between the Father and the Son, this also places more emphasis on a family environment within a kingdom setting. For this reason, when Jesus made the statement in John Chapter 14, He was speaking from this perspective.

1. Let not your heart be troubled: ye believe in God, believe also in me.

2. In my Father's house are many mansions: if it were not so, I would have told you. I go to prepare a place for you.

3. And if I go and prepare a place for you, I will come again, and receive you unto myself; that where I am, there ye may be also. (John 14:1-3)

Based on personal desires, coupled with a misinterpretation of Scripture, it is easy to use this passage to support the notion of mansions in heaven. However, this doctrine has been manufactured from reading the above passage in isolation. Therefore, to discover the proper perspective of John Chapter 14, it has to be discussed based on the context of the entire Gospel of John. Additionally, this chapter represents a portion of a *passage context,* which exists within a *book context.* Unfortunately, as a result of interpreting John Chapter 14 without consideration for its "contextual setting," Jesus' statement regarding mansions has been misconstrued.

As previously mentioned, each of the Gospels portrays Jesus from a different perspective. For example, based on their specific focus, Matthew and Luke contain genealogies, which reveal Jesus' earthly lineage. Matthew, in confirming Him as King and the One to fulfill the promise, begins His genealogy with David and Abraham. However, Luke, in affirming Him as the Son of man offers His complete heritage concluding with Adam. Mark, on the other hand, because it depicts Jesus as a servant, omits the genealogy as it is not fitting for a servant. Finally, the Gospel of John with its emphasis on Jesus as the Son of God bypasses His earthly heritage and instead, focuses on His eternal existence.

1. In the beginning was the Word, and the Word was with God, and the Word was God.
2. The same was in the beginning with God.
3. All things were made by him; and without him was not any thing made that was made.
4. In him was life; and the life was the light of men.
5. And the light shineth in darkness; and the darkness comprehended it not.
6. There was a man sent from God, whose name was John.
7. The same came for a witness, to bear witness of the Light, that all men through him might believe.
8. He was not that Light, but was sent to bear witness of that Light.
9. That was the true Light, which lighteth every man that cometh into the world.
10. He was in the world, and the world was made by him, and the world knew him not.
11. He came unto his own, and his own received him not.
12. But as many as received him, to them gave he power to become the sons of God, even to them that believe on his name:
13. Which were born, not of blood, nor of the will of the flesh, nor of the will of man, but of God.
14. And the Word was made flesh, and dwelt among us, (and we beheld his glory, the glory as of the only begotten of the Father,) full of grace and truth.

15. John bare witness of him, and cried, saying, This was he of whom I spake, He that cometh after me is preferred before me: for he was before me.
16. And of his fulness have all we received, and grace for grace.
17. For the law was given by Moses, but grace and truth came by Jesus Christ.
18. No man hath seen God at any time; the only begotten Son, which is in the bosom of the Father, he hath declared him. (John1:1-18)

From the onset of the book, rather than focusing on the substance of the kingdom, John begins with the substance of the Son of the kingdom. To convey the nature of Jesus Christ and to establish His eternal existence, the Gospel of John begins with the phrase, "In the beginning was the Word." Unlike the other Gospels that begin with Jesus' birth, John immediately introduces Jesus as the Word. In simple terms, His designation as the Word means that He is the very embodiment of everything spoken by God throughout the ages. This includes every promise, decree, covenant, and the overall pronouncement of His purpose. Furthermore, Jesus came not just *to fulfill* what God said but *as the fulfillment* of what God said (Matthew 5:17). He came as the fulfillment of God's purpose. This is why in referring to Him, Hebrews 10:7 says, "He came in the volume of the book." The volume of the book or the entirety of the Old Testament is fulfilled in the person of Jesus Christ.

Also, it should be noted there is no distinction between who God is and what He says. When it comes to God, there is no difference between His Word and who He is. His Word represents the very substance of His character. This may be difficult for us to grasp because sometimes when we say things or make promises, it is separate from who we are. When this occurs, it means we have no integrity or wholeness; we are divided. However, when God makes a promise, He *is* the very essence of the words He speaks. For instance, when He made the promise to Abraham, Scripture says He swore by Himself, and He became the confirmation for what He promised (Hebrews 6:13-18).

After establishing the preexistence of Christ, John 1:14 says that the Word was made flesh or Christ came as the personification of the Word of God. The very substance and character of God came in human form. Moreover, John adds that they took notice of Him or beheld His glory. This sets the premise that the visible manifestation of the Word of God is *always* glory. Hence, as sons of God, if we have His Word inside of us, it will always be evident.

As it pertains to Jesus and the sons of God, what does glory look like? What did John and the others see? The passage says that the glory He exhibited was that of the only begotten of the Father full of grace and truth.

The glory of God is always recognizable because it is always manifested as grace and truth. In short, grace is the reflection of God's influence in our lives. It is the observable evidence of the effectiveness of His Word by the way we live. Grace is simply the character of the Word of God on display. Truth is the genuine essence of something or corresponding to the original standard. Thus, as opposed to types and shadows, Christ reflected the very substance or nature of God and His purpose (Hebrews 11:1). He was the visible manifestation of the Word of God and the express image of the Father (Hebrews 1:3). Based on this scriptural example, glory is defined as *reflecting the inward working of God's influence (Word), possessing His nature, and being aligned with His purpose.* Consequently, as a son, if I am not walking in His purpose or allowing the Word to have its effectual work in me, there is no glory.

To qualify Jesus' position in relation to the Father, the Gospel of John exclusively uses the words "only begotten." The term "only begotten" is the Greek word *monogenes,* which is a combination of two words: *monos,* meaning only or alone and *genos,* meaning the same nature, kind, or species. Accordingly, "only begotten" means the only one of the family or the only one of the same stock in the relationship between the Father to the Son. Therefore, John presents Jesus as the Son who is the only offspring of the Father.

It should be noted that none of the other Gospels use the term "only begotten," which further expresses the theme of the book: Father-Son relationship. By this statement, John not only introduces us to the Father, but he also says Christ is of the same nature as the Father.

Notice what John 1:18 says, "No man hath seen God at any time; the only begotten Son, which is in the bosom of the Father, He hath declared Him." What precisely is this verse referring to? In harmony with the context of the chapter, this verse has nothing to do with actual, visual manifestations of God. Scripture tells us He was seen by Moses (Exodus 33:18-23) and Ezekiel (Ezekiel Chapter 1). Isaiah also had visions of Him (Isaiah 6:1-13).

Keep in mind that the context of John Chapter 1 is that the Word, which not only encompasses what God says but also who He is, took on flesh. As a result, for the first time, humanity had a visible manifestation of the character and substance of God. This is referred to as glory and the exhibition of it was one of grace and truth. Until Christ came, no man had fully seen the character of God on display. This is why the very essence of who God is (the Word) came in flesh form to demonstrate who He is, so we can pattern our lives after Him. Hence, *Jesus* told Philip in John 14:9, "He that hath seen me hath seen the Father." In other words, "As a Son, I am a visible representation of the Father."

Before Christ came, humanity's appreciation of God, for the most part, was in an abstract form. In fact, we did not have an intimate relationship with Him. Humanity's acquaintance with God only involved external performances. Hebrews 9:10 says these all involved carnal or fleshly ordinances until the time of reformation. Furthermore, His association with us was more aligned with attributes such as Creator, Lord, Deliverer, Shepherd, Protector, and so forth. However, when Jesus came, He introduced God as the Father, which also paved the way for humanity to become sons. Hence John 1:12 says, "But as many as received him, to them gave he power to become the sons of God, even to them that believe on his name."

Jesus brought the reality of a relationship with the Father. For humanity to become familiar with God as *Father,* Jesus the Son came to declare Him unto us. Jesus was able to reveal the Father unto us, not just because He is the very substance of the Father, but He was also in the bosom of the Father. The word "bosom" signifies an extremely close or intimate relationship or someone who is a partaker of the same. Thus, it signifies Jesus as one who is in a close relationship with the Father and understands His character and purpose. Throughout the Gospel of John, Jesus portrays Himself as a Son and provides the blueprint of the Father-Son relationship whose purpose is one with the Father.

FATHER-SON RELATIONSHIP

Just as humanity was not accustomed to God in the capacity of a Father, we were also not familiar with how to function as sons. Therefore, the Gospel of John places considerable emphasis on Jesus as the Son of God and shows how as a Son, He provides the perfect example of how sons of the kingdom behave or function. In its entirety, it is a Gospel, which by practical example serves as a blueprint for our relationship with the Father. In tune with the context of the book, Jesus refers to God as "the Father" or "My Father" an astonishing 108 times in the Gospel of John alone. He refers to Himself as "the Son of God" or simply "the Son" 30 times. By contrast, in the Gospels of Matthew, Mark, and Luke combined, He refers to God as "the Father" a total of only 57 times and refers to Himself as "the Son of God or "the Son" only 34 times. Therefore, John is convincingly dedicated to conveying a Father-Son relationship.

In order for humanity to have an appreciation of who God is, the Son declared the Father unto us. Additionally, in emphasizing the relationship between Himself and the Father, and His dependency on Him, Jesus constantly says that He can of Himself do nothing. Furthermore, as a Son who is in close contact and communication with the Father, He states that He is not here to do His own will, but the will of the Father who sent Him.

> Then answered Jesus and said unto them, Verily, verily, I say unto you, The Son can do nothing of Himself, but what He seeth the Father do: for what things soever He doeth, these also doeth the Son likewise. (John 5:19)

> I can of mine own self do nothing: as I hear, I judge and my judgment is just; because I seek not mine own will, but the will of the Father which hath sent me. (John 5:30)

> But I have greater witness than that of John: for the works which the father hath given me to finish, the same works that I do, bear witness of me, that the Father hath sent me. (John 5:36)

> For I came down from heaven, not to do mine own will, but the will of Him that sent me. (John 6:38)

28. Then said Jesus unto them, When ye have lifted up the Son of man, then shall ye know that I am he, and that I do nothing of myself; but as my Father hath taught me, I speak these things.

29. And he that sent me is with me: the Father hath not left me alone; for I do always those things that please him. (John 8:28-29)

For I have not spoken of myself; but the Father which sent me, He gave me a commandment, what I should say, and what I should speak. (John 12:49)

Jesus' actions and statements serve as a model for all the sons of the Father and our relationship with Him. Overall, He demonstrated a steadfast commitment to the Father's will and purpose. Additionally, He also expressed a consistent dependency on the Father. As mentioned previously, John accentuates God as Father, placing significant emphasis on the relationship between the Father and the Son. This supports the position that Matthew, Mark, and Luke focus more on what the kingdom is. On the other hand, John places greater attention on the Father-Son relationship within a kingdom environment. In consideration of this concept, let's look at the word "father."

FATHER

The word "Father" is the Greek word *pater* that means the following:

- Generator or male ancestor
- A founder of a family

- The progenitor of a people
- One who imparts life and is committed to it
- One in intimate connection and relationship.
- One who has infused his own spirit into others, who actuates and governs their minds

Jesus' identification of God as Father changed the dynamics of the relationship between God and humanity. Based on the natural examples of the attributes associated with a father, this definitely conveyed a more meaningful connection. For instance, when we consider the titles associated with Yahweh, such as Creator, Deliverer, and Provider, and the characteristics of these titles, we realize these are all incorporated and expressed in the designation of "Father." However, unlike the other names, "Father" speaks of intimacy, inheritance, care, culture, heritage, family, and household. "Father," says I am all those things but even more because we are family. Consequently, the corresponding relationship to "Father" is that of sons, which is a generic term that includes both men and women. In relation to God's eternal purpose, this is the highest of all the designations that can be bestowed on believers. This title is also in harmony with our original identity.

From the beginning, God's original purpose was to place humanity in the position of a son (Luke 3:38). This emphasizes the fact that from the beginning, all God wanted was a family. When God created humanity and gave them dominion over the earth (Genesis 1:26), this created a kingdom environment. Therefore, based on God's original design, humanity belonged to both the kingdom of God and the family of God. In fact, there is always a connection between God's kingdom and His house. Hence, without being a member of His house or family, you cannot be a citizen of His kingdom. The reverse is also true.

However, after Adam sinned, humanity became estranged from both the kingdom of God and the family of God. Thus, when Jesus came and said that the kingdom of heaven was at hand (Matthew 4:17), this was a message of restoration to the kingdom of God and the house or family of God. After Jesus' declaration concerning the kingdom, He then taught the people the principles of the kingdom of God. Additionally, humanity had defaulted from being a son into being and acting like a servant. Subsequently, Christ came in the capacity of a Son to reintroduce us to the concept of sonship and demonstrate how we should behave. He came to reacquaint us with our original identity. From the perspective of genetics, "son" speaks to who we are and expresses our true essence.

THE PURPOSE OF A SON

In relation to a father, the purpose of a son is as follows:

- A son is one who is in the role of his father to fulfill the father's life and purpose
- A son is an extension and a representative of the father
- A son declares his father's generation

Clearly, it is no coincidence that Jesus came in the capacity of a Son. He came as an extension of the Father to fulfill His purpose. This is why Ephesians 3:11 confirms that God's eternal purpose was orchestrated through Christ. Furthermore, according to the purpose of sons, one of their responsibilities is to declare the father's generation or heritage. Hence, Scripture contains genealogies, as it indicates the "begetting" of a son by the father. Accordingly, it not only represents a historical record, but it also reveals a family connection.

In the case of Jesus, Matthew 3:23 says, "And Jesus himself began to be about thirty years of age, being (as was supposed) the son of Joseph, which was the son of Heli." However, Matthew 1:18-25 says Jesus was born of the Holy Spirit. Therefore, seeing that Joseph did not beget Jesus, He was not charged with the responsibility of declaring his generation. This is why in Luke 2:49 when His parents were looking for Him, Jesus said, "How is it that ye sought me? Wist (know) ye not that I must be about my Father's business?" In other words, based on my heritage, I am the Father's representative to fulfill His purpose.

In accordance with sons declaring the generation of their fathers, the question is asked in Isaiah 53:8, "Who shall declare His generation?" To put it another way, who shall represent Him and fulfill His purpose. Who by their actions will declare that they are His seed? This question was asked in reference to Jesus Christ because Isaiah saw His death. However, he did not see the sons or the many brethren who would declare His generation.

The word "declare" in the context of the passage means to speak, to produce, to bring forth, or to germinate. In practical terms, my son is able to declare my generation because he is born of my seed. This is why 1 Peter 1:23 in reference to salvation says that we are born again of incorruptible seed, by the Word of God. Genesis 1:11 establishes the principle that every seed produces after its own kind. Accordingly, in a reproductive sense, the seed is the carrier of the heritage, characteristics, culture, life, and essence of the father. In consideration of these genetic qualities, only those who are born of the Father's seed are capable of declaring His generation.

Romans 8:15 says it is by receiving the Holy Spirit or the Spirit of adoption that we can cry Abba, Father. This process is equivalent to receiving the incorruptible seed mentioned in 1 Peter 1:23. As sons of God, begotten of the Father or born of His seed, we are charged with declaring the generation of Jesus Christ. By the things that are said and done, the seed will inherently declare the heritage of the father. For example, in John 8:44, Jesus said to the Pharisees, "You are of your father the devil, and the lusts of your father ye will do. He was a murderer from the beginning, and abode not in the truth, because there is no truth in him, When he speaketh a lie, he speaketh of his own: for he is a liar and the father of it." As a principle, fatherhood will always be evident by the words and actions of the seed or offspring.

We live in a religious environment where it is fashionable or cliché to refer to God as Father. In addition, we also make reference (not from a creation perspective) that we are children of God. While it is true that God is Father, this only pertains to those who are born of His seed and declare His generation. In using a natural example, I am a father but only to those born of my seed or with whom I have an affinity. I have no such relationship with those not born of my seed. Seed denotes family and a family speaks of the descendants of a common ancestor.

With the principle message of the Gospel of John being a relationship with the Father, the book immediately announces that those who believe in Him have the privilege of becoming sons. However, the distinction of birth is abundantly clear. Natural birth is not the qualification for being a son of the Father, it requires being born of God or spiritual birth.

11. He came unto his own, and his own received him not.

12. But as many as received him, to them gave he power to become the sons of God, even to them that believe on his name:

13. Which were born, not of blood, nor of the will of the flesh, nor of the will of man, but of God. (John 1:11-13)

This is in harmony with the conversation between Jesus and Nicodemus in John 3:5-7:

5. Jesus answered, Verily, verily, I say unto thee, Except a man be born of water and of the Spirit, he cannot enter into the kingdom of God.

6. That which is born of the flesh is flesh; and that which is born of the Spirit is spirit.

7.   Marvel not that I said unto thee, Ye must be born again.

As mentioned in my book *God's Eternal Purpose Volume Two*, being a son is more than just being an offspring. It represents a person who is an extension and representative of the Father to fulfill His life and purpose. Based on this premise, being a son is not limited to being born again but involves active participation in the fulfillment of God's purpose, which is the establishment of His kingdom. So in essence, *the relationship between the Father and sons denotes a family or the Father's house.* Hence, a son is responsible for the continuation of the father's house. This discussion catapults us into our next discussion on the Father's house, which is tabled in Chapter 4.

CHAPTER FOUR

The Father's House

WHAT IS THE FATHER'S HOUSE?

In John 14:2, when Jesus used the phrase, "My Father's house," what precisely was He referring to? Undoubtedly, the answer to this question holds the key to this entire discussion. Hence, once we determine what the Father's house is, this sets the parameter for the entire chapter. For the most part, the answer to this question based on tradition and assumption is heaven. However, part of the challenge with this response is that it represents a limited perspective of what a house entails. Additionally, this conclusion is made without considering the context of the book.

Keep in mind that the principal message of John is the kingdom of God but from a family perspective. Therefore, when Jesus used the term, Father's house, it was based on this premise. Recall from the previous chapter that the focus of the book is a Father-Son relationship. Therefore, Jesus coming in the capacity of a Son, and His reference to God as Father, means He also came representing a household or family. As the only begotten Son of the Father, He came as the representative of His Father's house with the responsibility of building and expanding it.

Also, notice that during this discussion, Jesus never used the word "heaven" in reference to the Father's house. According to Scripture, heaven is referred to as the place where God is (Joshua 2:11, Ecclesiastes 5:2, Matthew 6:9), His dwelling place (1 Kings 8:30), and His throne (Isaiah 66:1, Acts 7:49, Revelation 4:2). However, based on a careful examination of the Scriptures, heaven is never referred to as "the Father's house." To be clear, this is not a conclusion based on semantics but on the principles of rightly dividing the Word of God. In fact, in terms of direct mention, Jesus deliberately referred to the temple as the Father's house in John 2:16. Certainly, this reference creates a dynamic perspective for this discussion. However, this will be explained in detail later in the chapter once a good foundation is established.

HOUSE DEFINED

Throughout Scripture, the word "house" is used to describe the following:

- A dwelling place
- An individual or body
- Those belonging to the same household (family)
- A family of descendants as an organized body (nation)
- One's entire property

Let's look at several scriptures that support some of the above definitions of the word "house." As it pertains to an individual or our earthly bodies, 2 Corinthians 5:1 says, "For we know that if our *earthly house of this tabernacle* were dissolved, we have a building of God, *an house not made with hands*, eternal in the heavens." "House," therefore, can refer to our physical bodies as the dwelling places of our human spirits. By the same measure, it can also refer to the immortal bodies believers will receive during the first resurrection. Additionally, "house" can denote an entire family as in the case of Noah and Joshua.

In Genesis 7:1 after Noah had finished building the ark, the Lord said unto him, "Come thou and all *thy house* into the ark; for thee have I seen righteous before me in this generation." Moreover, in Joshua 24:15, Joshua said, "As for me and *my house*, we will serve the LORD." Also, as noted in Proverbs 6:31, "house" can be used to represent the wealth or substance that someone possesses meaning their entire property. Additionally, "house" can be attributed to an entire nation as in the case of Israel. In Exodus 16:31, the Israelites as a people are referred to as the "house of Israel" or the "house of Jacob" in Exodus 19:3. Furthermore, Hebrews Chapter 3, in referring to the nation of Israel, as well as the church, uses the word "house" to categorize both groups of people. Notice specifically that Hebrews 3:6 while referring to the church, uses the phrase, "house of Christ," which also represents His family.

1. Wherefore, holy brethren, partakers of the heavenly calling, consider the Apostle and High Priest of our profession, Christ Jesus;

2. Who was faithful to him that appointed him, as also Moses was faithful in all his house.

3. For this man was counted worthy of more glory than Moses, inasmuch as he who hath builded the house hath more honour than the house.

4. For every house is builded by some man; but he that built all things is God.

5. And Moses verily was faithful in all his house, as a servant, for a testimony of those things which were to be spoken after;

6. But Christ as a son over his own house; whose house are we, if we hold fast the confidence and the rejoicing of the hope firm unto the end. (Hebrews 6:1-6)

Based on a consensus of the definition, the word "house" expresses the notion of family or household inclusive of its possessions. It is definitely not limited to a physical structure or building. To further validate this position, the word "house" in John 14:2 is the Greek word *oikia,* which means:

- A dwelling
- Household or family
- Property or wealth

Therefore, Jesus is essentially saying, "In my Father's family or in my household, there are many mansions or dwelling places." Furthermore, He was also taking into account the substance of the house and all its possessions. Hence, when Jesus spoke of the Father's house, He was actually introducing or rather, reintroducing humanity to the family of God and His fullness.

As mentioned in my book *God's Eternal Purpose Volume One*, a house is an identifiable body of people with a common culture, name, governing influence, values, and nature. It is distinguished based on shared traits or identities. Within every family, there are recognizable characteristics and tendencies, which distinguish it from other families. Throughout the Gospels, when Jesus spoke of the culture of the kingdom of heaven, He was actually talking about the nature and identity of His family or the Father's house.

With the contrasting statements of "ye have heard," followed by, "but I say unto you," He was essentially highlighting the differences or the values between two distinct houses. One was the house of Israel with the governing influence of the law and the other was His house with the governing influence of the kingdom of God. Not only was Jesus introducing humanity to the family of God, but He was also doing so within the confines of a kingdom concept. This is no ordinary family or house but one of royalty. Hence, 1 Peter 2:9 refers to the family of God as a chosen generation and a royal priesthood.

On that point, in John Chapter 14, Jesus was simultaneously presenting two dynamics. One was the family of God and the other was His kingdom. However, as stated, it is important to understand that the two entities are not separate from each other; they are interdependent. In relation to the kingdom, the house, which consists of the family, is an essential component of the kingdom. Therefore, as it pertains to the kingdom of God, recall the basic principle is that in *order to be a part or inheritor of the kingdom, you have to be a member of the house.* Conversely, without being a member of the house, you cannot be a part or an inheritor of the kingdom. Consequently, to be a part of the house and be counted for an inheritance, you have to be a son.

GOD'S ORIGINAL PURPOSE: A FAMILY OF SONS

God's concept of establishing a family or His house is nothing new. It was His original purpose from the beginning. The objective of the Father has always been to have a family, particularly a family of sons. As mentioned, the word "son" is all-encompassing, including both men and women as it is used to illustrate what a son represents. Luke 3:38 says that when God created Adam, He made him in the capacity of a son. Adam bore God's image and likeness. Furthermore, as God was extending His kingdom influence to the earth, He gave both man and woman dominion or kingdom rule over the earth (Genesis 1:26). This establishes the parameter that it was the Father's intent not only to create a family or a house but one within a kingdom environment.

The instruction in Genesis 1:28 to be fruitful, multiply, and replenish the earth, served as the mandate to create more sons for the kingdom, thereby expanding the family of God. However, when man sinned, not only was there a transfer from one kingdom to another, we also became estranged from the family of God and His house. Sin alienated us from God, which included both the Father's house and His kingdom.

As mentioned, the principle is that *our kingdom affiliation is also in alignment with our family relationship.* Therefore, it is impossible to make the claim that you are a part of the kingdom of God without being a member of His family.

Based on God's original purpose, along with the above principle, Scripture creates a parallel between the first Adam of the garden of Eden and the last Adam who is Jesus Christ (1 Corinthians 15:45, Romans 5:12-14). In this instance, the name "Adam" conveys the message that each one is a representative figure carrying the seed for two generations of people, two groups of families, and two distinct kingdoms. See the chart below:

First Adam	Last Adam
• son of God (created)	• Son of God (Only Begotten)
• Image and likeness of God	• Express image of God's person (substance)
• Kingdom mandate	• Kingdom mandate
• Represented the family of God	• Came as the representative of the Father's house or family
• Mandate to produce more sons for the kingdom	• Through His death, He brings many sons into glory. He is the firstborn among many brethren.
• Sin resulted in seed becoming corruptible.	• Came with the incorruptible seed

▪ Through sin alienated humanity from the family of God	▪ Through His death, He restores humanity to the family of God.
▪ As a result of disobedience, he produced citizens of the kingdom of darkness.	▪ Produced citizens of the kingdom of God

Therefore, when Christ came as the last Adam, He not only came in the capacity of a Son, but He also came as the *only begotten* Son of the Father. Also, He did not just come in the image and likeness of God, but He also came as the express image or the very substance of the Father (Hebrews 1:3). Furthermore, He not only came with the same mandate as the first Adam, but He also came to *reestablish* the family of God on Earth in a kingdom environment. For this reason, His platform from the onset was, "Repent: for the kingdom of heaven is at hand."

The prefix "re" means to go back or to do something again. Hence, Jesus' message was, "Change your mind for God's original idea is being reintroduced." Thus, the message He taught was directed at changing or realigning the minds of the people to the culture of the kingdom of heaven. Not only was Jesus reintroducing the kingdom of God on Earth, but also included in that was the commission of restoration. Christ was charged with the responsibility of restoring humanity to the Father's house or family of God and His kingdom. To accomplish this required a sacrifice. However, the sacrifices of the law only provided temporary redemption for sin.

1. For the law having a shadow of good things to come, and not the very image of the things, can never with those sacrifices which they offered year by year continually make the comers thereunto perfect.

2. For then would they not have ceased to be offered? because that the worshippers once purged should have had no more conscience of sins.

3. But in those sacrifices there is a remembrance again made of sins every year.

4. For it is not possible that the blood of bulls and of goats should take away sins.

5. Wherefore when he cometh into the world, he saith, Sacrifice and offering thou wouldest not, but a body hast thou prepared me. (Hebrews 10:1-5)

To provide eternal redemption and eternal inheritance for humanity (Hebrews 9:12-15), Christ came in the fashion of a man and offered Himself once and for all. The combination of eternal redemption and eternal inheritance speaks of reinstatement into the family of God or the Father's house and by extension, the inheritance of the kingdom of God. In connecting this with Christ's mandate to reestablish the family of God on Earth, Hebrews 2:10-17 says:

10. For it became him, for whom are all things, and by whom are all things, *in bringing many sons unto glory,* to make the captain of their salvation perfect through sufferings.

11. For both he that sanctifieth and they who are sanctified are all of one: for which cause *he is not ashamed to call them brethren,*
12. *Saying, I will declare thy name unto my brethren,* in the midst of the church will I sing praise unto thee.
13. And again, I will put my trust in him. And again, *Behold I and the children which God hath given me.*
14. Forasmuch then as the children are partakers of flesh and blood, he also himself likewise took part of the same; that through death he might destroy him that had the power of death, that is, the devil;
15. And deliver them who through fear of death were all their lifetime subject to bondage.
16. For verily he took not on him the nature of angels; but he took on him the seed of Abraham.
17. Wherefore in all things it behoved him to be made like unto his brethren, that he might be a merciful and faithful high priest in things pertaining to God, to make reconciliation for the sins of the people.

The above passage offers tremendous consistency with the fact that Jesus was charged with building and expanding the Father's house consisting of sons of the kingdom. Notice the deliberate usage of the following phrases in the passage:

• Bringing many sons into glory
• He is not ashamed to call them brethren

- I will declare thy name (the Father's name) unto my brethren
- I and the children, which God hath given Me

Among similar passages in the Bible, this one, in particular, clearly conveys the purpose of Christ. It speaks of incorporating humanity into the family of God in the capacity of sons, regarding us as brothers. With the reintroduction of the kingdom of God on Earth, this also meant adoption into the family of God. This was accomplished by the Spirit of adoption or the incorruptible seed, which genetically makes God our Father. As the two are inherently connected, because we are members of the Father's house, we are consequently heirs of the kingdom of God.

15. For ye have not received the spirit of bondage again to fear; but ye have received the Spirit of adoption, whereby we cry, Abba, Father.
16. The Spirit itself beareth witness with our spirit, that we are the children of God:
17. And if children, then heirs; heirs of God, and joint-heirs with Christ; if so be that we suffer with him, that we may be also glorified together. (Romans 8:15-17)

The word "adoption" is the Greek word *huiothesia*. It is a combination of two words, *huios* meaning "son" and *tithemi* meaning "placement." Therefore, it means the placement or installation of a son. The word "adoption" means the voluntary act of legally taking a child and caring for that child as your own. Scripture uses the word "adoption" in reference to us as sons of God because it is a formal and legal declaration that God is our Father (Abba), and we have complete rights as children including that of inheritance.

THE TEMPLE AS THE FATHER'S HOUSE

To get a more comprehensive understanding of the Father's house, let's look at it from the perspective of the temple. When Jesus referred to the temple as the Father's house, what exactly did He mean, and how does that factor into this discussion? To determine that, it is necessary to go back to its inception in Scripture.

In 2 Samuel Chapter 7, David, while sitting in his house of cedar and reflecting on where the Ark of God was, expressed a desire to build a house for the Lord. By comparison, the Ark of God (which represented the presence of the Lord) dwelled in curtains. Therefore, David wanted to build a temple or a permanent structure for the Lord to dwell in. However, the Lord, through the prophet Nathan, made certain promises to David, which is also referred to as the Davidic covenant.

11. And as since the time that I commanded judges to be over my people Israel, and have caused thee to rest from all thine enemies. Also the LORD telleth thee that he will make thee an house.
12. And when thy days be fulfilled, and thou shalt sleep with thy fathers, I will set up thy seed after

thee, which shall proceed out of thy bowels, and I will establish his kingdom.

13. He shall build an house for my name, and I will stablish the throne of his kingdom for ever.

14. I will be his father, and he shall be my son. If he commit iniquity, I will chasten him with the rod of men, and with the stripes of the children of men:

15. But my mercy shall not depart away from him, as I took it from Saul, whom I put away before thee.

16. And thine house and thy kingdom shall be established for ever before thee: thy throne shall be established for ever. (2 Samuel 7:11-16)

David's initial request was to build a house for the Lord. However, the Lord said to him, "I will instead build you a house." Whereas David's request was to build a physical house or temple, the Lord's promise to him was in reference to the formation of a family or household. Scripture refers to this as the house of David or the tabernacle of David. Moreover, because David was a king, it made the house or family royal and all those associated with it have the distinction of royalty. The house, therefore, serves as the foundation for what the Lord wanted to do, which was to establish His kingdom forever.

After addressing the establishment of the house or family, God said He will set up David's seed and establish His kingdom. Notice 2 Samuel 7:16 says the house and the kingdom shall be established forever. This further supports the fact that there is always a direct correlation between these two entities: the house and the kingdom.

When we take a closer look at the precise details of the covenant, it is apparent that it has a two-fold significance in that it involves two individuals. Hence, the term "seed of David" is in reference to both Solomon and Jesus Christ who is also referred to in Matthew 1:1 as the seed of David. Notice as it pertains to both of them, the passage says, "He shall build a house for my name." Therefore, both Solomon and Jesus, who are the sons of David, are charged with the responsibility of *building the house of God*.

In the first instance, "building a house for the Lord" points to Solomon building the temple of God as recorded in 1 Kings 6. The temple served as the dwelling place of God; hence, Jesus specifically referred to it as the Father's house in John 2:13-16. Prior to the temple, the tabernacle was the residence or dwelling place of God (Exodus 25:17-22; 33:7-11). In this regard, Solomon was a type of Christ as they both are categorized as "the builders of the house of God." Whereas Solomon was commissioned to build the physical temple or house of God, Christ is charged with the building of a spiritual house and household (family). To this point, there are also several passages of Scripture, which speak to our bodies being temples and believers being the temple of God, as well as the house of God.

19. Jesus answered and said unto them, *Destroy this temple, and in three days I will raise it up.*
20. Then said the Jews, Forty and six years was this temple in building, and wilt thou rear it up in three days?
21. *But he spake of the temple of his body.* (John 2:19-21)

What? Know ye not that *your body is the temple of the Holy Ghost which is in you*, which ye have of God, and ye are not your own? (1 Corinthians 6:19)

Ye also, as lively stones, *are built up a spiritual house*, an holy priesthood, to offer up spiritual sacrifices, acceptable to God by Jesus Christ. (1 Peter 2:5)

But Christ as a son over his own house; whose house are we, if we hold fast the confidence and the rejoicing of the hope firm unto the end. (Hebrews 3:6)

18. For through him we both have access by one Spirit unto the Father.
19. Now therefore ye are no more strangers and foreigners, but fellowcitizens with the saints, and of the household of God;
20. And are built upon the foundation of the apostles and prophets, Jesus Christ himself being the chief corner stone;
21. In whom all the building fitly framed together groweth unto an holy temple in the Lord:
22. In whom ye also are builded together for an habitation of God through the Spirit. (Ephesians 2:18-22)

Therefore, with the sons of God being His dwelling place or His temple, we are also referred to as His house.

Hence, as believers, we are the house of God individually and collectively. Additionally, with His Spirit dwelling in us, this makes us His sons and thus, His family.

Now that we have determined based on Scripture that the Father's house pertains to the family of God, we are poised to better understand the context and perspective of mansions. Based on the premise that Jesus is responsible for "building the house of God or the Father's family," He then says in John 14:2, "In my Father's house are many mansions."

CHAPTER FIVE

The Passage Context

As we continue our comprehensive discussion of the Gospel of John and its passage context, there are three important questions to be answered that are pivotal to this discussion:

1. What did Jesus mean when He said, "I go to prepare a place for you?"
2. What was He referring to when He said, "I will come again and receive you unto myself?"
3. What was the implication when Jesus said, "Where I am, there you will be also?"

THE PASSAGE CONTEXT: JOHN CHAPTER 11 TO 17

It is important to note that Jesus did not make these statements after His resurrection or before His ascension to heaven. For if that were the case, the context of the passage would be considerably different. Instead, He made them prior to His death on the cross.

What did He mean by these comments and what were the circumstances surrounding these promises? To make that determination, we would have to take the entire "passage context" into consideration. Recall from Chapter 1 that the principle of a "passage context" says that verses of a particular chapter must not be interpreted in isolation from the chapter, passage, or book under consideration. The critical error that many make when reading John Chapter 14 is a disregard for the passage context in which the chapter exists. This has led to interpreting Chapter 14 in isolation resulting in a misguided doctrine.

John Chapter 14 belongs to a passage context dedicated to highlighting the significance of Jesus' death. In earnest, the passage extends from the latter portion of John Chapter 11 and continues through Chapter 17. Therefore, in order to have the correct context and perspective of Scripture regarding any of these chapters, the entire passage has to be carefully examined. Nevertheless, the conclusions of the passage are still subject to the framework of the "book context," for the entire Gospel of John sets the parameter. By reviewing the passage in detail, we will also be provided with the answers to the preceding three questions.

1. I GO TO PREPARE A PLACE FOR YOU

In my Father's house are many mansions: if it were not so, I would have told you. I go to prepare a place for you. (John 14:2)

As we have determined, the term, "the Father's house," refers to His family or household and has nothing to do with heaven. Additionally, the proper context of the Father's house being established contributes to a better understanding of the word "mansions." The word "mansions" is the Greek word *mone*, which means the following:

- Habitation
- Abode
- A Staying (Residence)
- Abiding
- A Dwelling (The Holy Spirit Dwelling Inside Believers And Believers Dwelling In The Father)

Based on the proper context of the Father's house and mansions, this changes the perspective of Jesus' statement, "I go to prepare a place for you." In truth, Jesus was saying that within His Father's household or family, there are many places for you to dwell. However, the privilege of dwelling in the Father's house is reserved strictly for sons. Consequently, in order for us to become sons, Jesus says, "I go to prepare a place for you." Clearly, there is a connection between becoming sons and Jesus *going to prepare a place for us* in the Father's house.

When Jesus said, "I go to prepare a place for you," He was speaking of what would be accomplished through His death. However, based on a misinterpretation of John 14:2, there is a perspective that Jesus went to heaven to start a building project consisting of mansions. Jesus' death and resurrection made it possible for humanity to become sons of God or members of the Father's family. Consequently, the place that He was going to prepare was the ability and privilege of the Father dwelling in us and we in Him. This is what the word "mansions" refers to.

Throughout this passage, Jesus constantly uses the term "going away" to signify His death (John 14:28, John 16:7). Again, as a matter of scriptural soundness, this entire conversation occurs *before* Jesus' death and not *after* His resurrection. For if it was after His resurrection, then the context would be different. To have a better appreciation for the complete discussion, let us examine the details of the entire passage context.

In John Chapter 11 after Jesus brought Lazarus back to life, the chief priests and the Pharisees gathered together and determined that if they allowed Jesus to continue doing miracles, the Romans would come and take away their place and nation. Evidently, Jesus was a threat to their positions, religion, and way of life. Consequently, Caiaphas the high priest said, "It is expedient for us, that one man should die for the people, and that the whole nation perish not." Based on the premise established in the law pertaining to the Passover, and in his position as the high priest, he was essentially identifying Christ as the Passover or the Lamb of God (John

1:29, 1 Corinthians 5:7) who should taste death for every man (Hebrews 2:9).

Under the law, the purpose of the Passover was for the redemption of the people and atonement for sin. The word "redeem" means the payment of a price to recover from the power of another or simply to ransom. When Adam sinned, humanity was subjected to another power or kingdom, which Colossians 1:13 refers to as the power of darkness. Simultaneously, we also lost our relationship with God and were subjugated to another house and father. Humanity's place in the Father's house was lost and the price of "preparing a place" for us or reinstating us in the Father's house was death. Therefore, Christ came as the Passover to redeem us to the kingdom of God and restore us to the Father's house.

13. Who hath delivered us from the power of darkness, and hath translated us into the kingdom of his dear Son:
14. In whom we have redemption through his blood, even the forgiveness of sins. (Colossians 1:13-14)

In effect, Christ's act of redemption also has the power of atonement. From a human perspective, I could redeem you, but I don't necessarily have to restore you. In general terms, redemption says I paid the price to ransom you from the power that held you captive. However, redemption coupled with atonement speaks of something more significant. The word "atone" means to reconcile, which is to reestablish a close relationship, to reunite, or to restore harmony. It is a condition that says the act of offense never occurred; therefore, there is a complete restoration. This speaks of the reinstatement of our status as sons in accordance with God's original purpose.

Sin alienated us from God and made us His enemies. Therefore, Christ was not just redeeming humanity; He was also restoring us to our rightful position in the kingdom of God and as members of His house.

> 21. And you, that were sometime alienated and ene-mies in your mind by wicked works, yet now hath he reconciled
> 22. In the body of his flesh through death, to present you holy and unblameable and unreproveable in his sight. (Colossians 1:21-22)

> 10. For if, when we were enemies, we were reconciled to God by the death of his Son, much more, being reconciled, we shall be saved by his life.
> 11. And not only so, but we also joy in God through our Lord Jesus Christ, by whom we have now received the atonement. (Romans 5:10-11)

In consideration of Christ's role in redemption and atonement, the high priest made a profound statement in John 11:51-52. In effect, the passage indicates that he was actually prophesying when he said that Christ should die *for the purpose of gathering together in* _one_ *the children of God who were scattered abroad.* Unbeknownst to him, he was essentially fulfilling his role as high priest as prescribed in the law. Furthermore, this statement of "gathering together in one" sets the stage for the entire dialogue of the passage context.

Keep in mind that the purpose of Jesus' death as conveyed in the chapter is to join together or join in one those who were previously separated. In truth, this is the same message of restoration, reconciliation, and unity (preparing a place in the Father's house). Furthermore, the word "children" in John 11:52 is the same Greek word *teknon* from which we get the word "sons" in John 1:12. Hence, the communication of the verse reinforces that the purpose of Jesus' death is for the reunification of sons with the Father or to bring the sons back into the Father's house and consequently, the kingdom. Throughout the remainder of this passage context, the theme of unity with the Father constantly reverberates.

Based on this foundation, in John Chapter 12, six days before the Passover, while at Bethany, Mary anoints the feet of Jesus in preparation for His death (John 12:7). This is followed by Jesus' entry into Jerusalem where the people held palm branches and cried, "Hosanna: Blessed is the King of Israel that cometh in the name of the Lord." Further illustrating the purpose of His death, Jesus said in John 12:24, "Except a corn of wheat fall into the ground and die, it abideth alone: but if it die, it bringeth forth much fruit." The term "much fruit" is in the same context as bringing many sons into glory, which is in alignment with the purpose of Christ; that is, reconciling humanity with the Father.

Additionally, in signifying the type of death He would die, which was on the cross, Jesus says in John 12:32, "And I, if I be lifted up from the Earth will draw all men unto me." Of note, this verse has nothing to do with lifting up Jesus in song or worship. He was simply indicating the type of death He was going to die. Moreover, the phrase "draw all men unto me" indicates that as a result of His death, He would have the power or influence to lead men unto Him. The same word "draw" is used in John 6:44 where Jesus says, "No man can come to me, except the Father which hath sent me draws him: and I will raise him up at the last day." Again, this is the same message of restoration, reconciliation, and unity with the Father. Therefore, the message of reconciliation with the Father is consistent from chapter to chapter and in agreement with the passage context.

John Chapter 13, in harmony with the passage context, advances the discussion with the conversation of the Passover.

> Now before the feast of the Passover, when Jesus knew that his hour was come that he should depart out of this world unto the Father, having loved his own which were in the world, he loved them unto the end. (John 13:1)

After supper, Jesus washed His disciples' feet. This was both a lesson in humility, as well as a foreshadowing act of His cleansing. During the latter part of the chapter, Jesus specifically refers to His death tabling it as "going away." When Peter asked Him where He was going, Jesus distinctly says, "You cannot follow me now but you shall follow me afterward."

> 31. Therefore, when he was gone out, Jesus said, Now is the Son of man glorified, and God is glorified in him.

32. If God be glorified in him, God shall also glorify him in himself, and shall straightway glorify him.

33. Little children, yet a little while I am with you. Ye shall seek me: and as I said unto the Jews, Whither I go, ye cannot come; so now I say to you.

34. A new commandment I give unto you, That ye love one another; as I have loved you, that ye also love one another.

35. By this shall all men know that ye are my disciples, if ye have love one to another.

36. Simon Peter said unto him, Lord, whither goest thou? Jesus answered him, Whither I go, thou canst not follow me now; but thou shalt follow me afterwards.

37. Peter said unto him, Lord, why cannot I follow thee now? I will lay down my life for thy sake.

38. Jesus answered him, Wilt thou lay down thy life for my sake? Verily, verily, I say unto thee, The cock shall not crow, till thou hast denied me thrice. (John 13:31-38)

In John Chapter 13, Jesus, while forecasting His death on the cross, also spoke of His betrayal and Peter's denial of Him. As a result of what He said, the disciples felt sad. To console them, He reiterated the purpose of His death. Recall that the purpose of His death was to create unity between the Father and humanity. Therefore, based on this context, He continues in Chapter 14 with words of comfort and says to His disciples, "Let not your heart be troubled."

In essence, He was saying, my death may seem like unpleasant news, but it is actually for your benefit. The purpose of my death is that it gives me the ability to prepare a mansion or a dwelling place for you in my Father's house or family. Jesus had to satisfy the requirements of redemption, which states that without the shedding of blood, there is no remission of sins or forgiveness (Hebrews 9:22). For this reason, to redeem humanity and restore us to the family of God, Jesus had to offer Himself as a sacrifice. This is why in reference to His death and what would follow, He said, "I go to prepare a place for you."

2. I WILL COME AGAIN AND RECEIVE YOU UNTO MYSELF

After speaking of the Father's house, mansions, and preparing a place for us, Jesus says in John 14:3, "And if I go and prepare a place for you, I will come again, and receive you unto myself." Once the proper context of John Chapter 14 has been established, the perspective changes from what is traditionally believed. Just as the term "going away" is not in reference to Jesus going to heaven, but to the cross, the phrase, "I will come again" neither points to the rapture nor His second advent. In fact, it specifically speaks of the benefits that would occur as a result of His death and His resurrection.

Based on the passage context, I reiterate that the framework for this entire exchange is concerning becoming one with the Father. Hence, immediately after Jesus makes the statement that He would come again and receive us unto

Himself, He speaks of the coming of the Holy Spirit. In other words, He explains how dwelling with the Father or becoming one with Him would be accomplished.

16. And I will pray the Father, and he shall give you another Comforter, <u>that he may abide with you for ever;</u>
17. Even the Spirit of truth; whom the world cannot receive, because it seeth him not, neither knoweth him: but ye know him; <u>for he dwelleth with you, and shall be in you.</u>
18. <u>I will not leave you comfortless: I will come to you.</u>
19. Yet a little while, and the world seeth me no more; but ye see me: because I live, ye shall live also.
20. <u>At that day ye shall know that I am in my Father, and ye in me, and I in you.</u> (John14:16-20)

After stating His own dwelling position of being in the Father and the Father being in Him, Jesus says that this same opportunity is being extended to you. This is the same as saying, "In my Father's house are many mansions, I go to prepare a place for you." How can the Father dwelling in us and us dwelling in the Father be accomplished? Jesus says He will send the Spirit of truth or the Holy Spirit to dwell in us. Therefore, when we receive the Holy Spirit, we are in Christ; He is in us, and we are also in the Father.

The tabernacle, or more specifically, the temple, which is referred to as the Father's house or the house of God was designed for God to dwell among His people and commune with them (Exodus 25:22). However, the intent of the Father was not just to "tabernacle" with humanity but for us to also "tabernacle" with Him. The temple represented God dwelling *with* us but this was external, as well as one-sided. Hence, through Christ, the Father was creating a way for Him to dwell *in* us and us *in* Him, thereby providing a perfect dwelling.

While the Father was "preparing a place for us," He was simultaneously preparing us as a place to dwell in. Therefore, with the Father dwelling in us, Scripture refers to our bodies or our "house" as the dwelling place of God or His temple (1 Corinthians 6:19). Furthermore, in John 14:23 Jesus says, "If a man loves me, he will keep my words: and my Father will love him, and will come unto him, and make our abode with him." The word "abode" in this passage is the same Greek word for mansions *mone* used in John 14:2. Therefore, this serves as an additional witness that Jesus' reference to "mansion" was directly associated with the Father dwelling in us and us dwelling in Him.

3. And if I go and prepare a place for you, I will come again, and receive you unto myself; that where I am, there ye may be also.
4. And whither I go ye know, and the way ye know.
5. Thomas saith unto him, Lord, we know not whither thou goest; and how can we know the way?
6. Jesus saith unto him, I am the way, the truth, and the life: no man cometh unto the Father, but by me. (John 14:3-6)

When Jesus said I will come again and receive you unto myself, He was referring to the coming of the Holy Spirit.

He was providing access to the Father as the builder of the Father's house; He is the way, the truth, and the life. He is the only one capable of drawing all men and uniting them with the Father

3. WHERE I AM THERE YE MAY BE ALSO

In reiterating John 14:3, Jesus says, "And if I go and prepare a place for you, I will come again, and receive you unto myself that where I am, there ye may be also." In maintaining the context of the conversation, Jesus is still referring to being members of the family of God and dwelling in the Father. Therefore, this is a statement of unity with Him and the Father.

In John 14:10-11, Jesus speaks of being in the Father and the Father being in Him. In other words, He was saying, as a Son, I dwell in the Father and the Father dwells in me. Therefore, in John Chapter 14, Jesus is basically providing a detailed description of what it is like to be in unity with the Father or to be one with Him. This is the encapsulation of His statement, "Where I am." Hence, after Jesus explains that this is where He is, the remainder of the chapter expounds on the phrase, "there ye may be also."

Jesus was fundamentally saying you can also be one with the Father just as I am. He was providing the ability for humanity to join Him and experience the same type of dwelling. However, how was this going to be accomplished?

When Jesus said, "I will come again, and receive you unto myself," He was referring to the coming of the Holy Spirit. In the first portion of John Chapter 14, Jesus speaks of dwelling in the Father and the Father dwelling in us (John 14:1-14). However, in the second portion of the chapter (John 14:15-31), He talks about the Comforter or the Holy Ghost abiding or dwelling with us. Hence, to get a complete understanding of what the chapter is saying, the connection has to be made between believers dwelling in the Father and the Holy Ghost dwelling in believers. The Holy Spirit dwelling in the sons of God is the fulfillment of John 14:3 where Jesus said, "I will come again and receive you unto myself; that where I am, there ye may be also." By virtue of the Holy Spirit dwelling in us, we simultaneously dwell in the Father. He is in us, and we are in Him. This speaks of unity dwelling. The Holy Spirit is the Spirit of adoption (Romans 8:15); therefore, when He dwells in us, we are adopted into the Father's house or His family.

Furthermore, in John 14:20, Jesus says, "At that day ye shall know that I am in my Father, ye in me, and I in you." To be clear, the day that He was referring to was when they received the Holy Spirit. Hence, John 14:20 describes the statement, "Where I am, there ye may be also." In other words, when you receive the Holy Ghost, you will be incorporated into the Father and you will be where I am also. This creates the perfect illustration of unity dwelling. John 14:23 reinforces this when it says that if we love Jesus and keep His words, the Father and Son will love us and come and make their abode or dwelling in us. As we have concluded, it is the same concept of mansions expressed in John 14:2

Contrary to popular doctrine, Jesus wasn't referring to heaven. In John 14:6, He was distinctly speaking about admittance to the Father and His house or unity with the Father. This was the reason He indicated He was the access or the way, the truth, and the life. As the one responsible for building the Father's house, He states that admittance to the Father is exclusively through Him.

ABIDE IN ME

In continuing with the message of the passage context, when we cross the threshold from John Chapter 14 into Chapter 15, the conversation remains the same. However, for some reason, John Chapter 15 is often read in complete isolation without considering what was said previously. When we read the Scriptures in a disconnected manner, the result is error and inaccurate doctrine. However, the chapter continues the discussion of dwelling in Christ and the Father dwelling in us. In other words, the impact of mansions is further explained in Chapter 15.

Take note that the word "abide" in John 15:4 speaks of remaining in Christ and is one of the definitions for the word mansions. To provide a practical example of dwelling in Him and what is required of the Father, Jesus compared Himself to a vine and the sons of the Father to branches. Therefore, dwelling in Him and He (the Holy Spirit) in us carries with it the responsibility of bearing fruit. Hence, while the church is concerned with physical buildings or mansions in heaven, the true essence of mansions or dwelling in the Father pertains to manifesting the glory of the Father or the character of God.

In the analogy, Jesus likens Himself to the vine, the Father as the vine-dresser, and the church as the branches. The job of the vine-dresser is to nurture, trim, or prune the vine to ensure it matures and produces fruit.

2. Every branch in me that beareth not fruit he taketh away: and every branch that beareth fruit, he purgeth it, that it may bring forth more fruit.
3. Now ye are clean through the word which I have spoken unto you.
4. Abide in me, and I in you. As the branch cannot bear fruit of itself, except it abide in the vine; no more can ye, except ye abide in me. (John 15:2-4)

This process of pruning is similar to chastisement mentioned in Hebrews 12:5-11, which is also designed to produce fruit in the sons of God. Hebrews 12:11 refers to it as the peaceable fruit of righteousness or righteous character.

ABIDING IN CHRIST INVOLVES PERSECUTION

After providing a practical illustration of abiding or dwelling in Him and all that entails, Jesus then pivots and tells His disciples to expect persecution. Persecution, therefore, is an automatic consequence of abiding in Christ. Hence, the concept of mansions also involves being mistreated for His name. This is why Jesus said in John 15:18, "If the world hate you, ye know that it hated me

before it hated you." Being in union with someone means that we are also subjected to the same things they endure. When we were in union or one with the world, the world loved us. However, because we are now one with the Father, the world hates us.

Furthermore, another result of abiding in Christ is testifying or bearing witness of Him. This includes not just what we say but it is also manifested in our characters. Recall that with God, there is no distinction between what He says and who He is or His character. He is the very essence of His Word. Therefore, Christ, being one with the Father testified of Him, not just in the words He said but also in His character. The Word was made flesh and manifested the glory of the Father (John 1:14). Similarly, bearing witness of Christ means that as believers we become the visible manifestation of who He is. Hence, Jesus said the purpose of the Holy Spirit is to bear witness of Him (John 15:26).

In continuing with the subject of persecution, Jesus says in John 16:1, "These things have I spoken unto you, that ye should not be offended." One of the definitions of the word "offended" is "to cause people to distrust and desert those they ought to trust and obey." Hence, Jesus was saying when persecution comes continue to trust in Me. Hence, the offense isn't necessarily directed at the oppressors but rather, toward the one with whom we are in unity. In order to explain the type of persecutions that will arise, Jesus provides two examples in John 16:2. First, He says they will put you out of the synagogue. Hence, the religious establishment will excommunicate you from their gatherings. Additionally, Jesus says they will kill you. Interestingly, He says those who kill

you will think they are doing the service of God. However, they are not one with the Father but rather, one with the world.

Jesus told His disciples all of these things to prepare them for the events that would occur after His departure. What is interesting is that up to that point, none of the disciples asked Jesus specifically where He was going (John 16:5). Even though He implied in John 12:32 what would happen to Him with the term "being lifted up," He didn't explicitly explain the means by which He was going away. Moreover, the reason they didn't ask where He was going was that sorrow had filled their hearts (John 16:6).

In John 16:16, He furthers the conversation with the statement, "A little while, and ye shall not see me: and again, a little while, and ye shall see me, because I go unto my Father." In this statement, He was foretelling His death, resurrection, and ascension to heaven with His blood for the redemption and atonement of humanity.

His disciples were oblivious to what He was referring to. Therefore, to prepare them for His death and its significance He said, "Ye shall lament, but the world shall rejoice: and ye shall be sorrowful, but your sorrow shall be turned into joy." To qualify His statement, He then provides a practical example of a woman who, while sorrowful during childbirth, is later joyful after delivering her child. As Jesus is still engaged in the same discourse regarding the purpose of His death, these statements are intended to support what He said in John 14:1, "Let not your heart be troubled."

JESUS' PRAYER OF UNITY

Finally, we get to John Chapter 17, which represents the end of the passage context for this discussion on unity with the Father. The chapter begins with the words, "These words spake Jesus, and lifted up his eyes to heaven, and said, Father, the hour is come; glorify thy Son, that thy Son also may glorify thee." Essentially, the chapter is dedicated to two specific things. First, Jesus offers a prayer that captures His purpose or the reason why He came. With what was on the threshold, He acknowledges He has finished the work He was given to do.

For the remainder of the chapter, the emphasis is placed on the purpose of His disciples. Therefore, while praying to the Father, He affirms that He has prepared them for His departure. As He was sending them out into the world, He also petitions the Father to keep and sanctify them. Moreover, Jesus makes it clear that the prayer wasn't solely for the disciples that were present with Him but actually for the entire church.

20. Neither pray I for these alone, but for them also which shall believe on me through their word;

21. That they all may be one; as thou, Father, art in me, and I in thee, that they also may be one in us: that the world may believe that thou hast sent me.

22. And the glory which thou gavest me I have given them; that they may be one, even as we are one:

23. I in them, and thou in me, that they may be made perfect in one; and that the world may know that thou hast sent me, and hast loved them, as thou hast loved me. (John 17:20-23)

As a great summary of the discussion, Jesus reintroduces the purpose of His death, which was stated throughout the passage context beginning in John Chapter 11. Recall that His objective was to "gather together in one the children of God" and "provide a dwelling place in the Father's house or family." In accordance with these precepts, Jesus reinforces the same concept with the message of unity in John Chapter 17. In using the identical language found in John Chapter 14, He speaks of the Father dwelling in believers and simultaneously believers dwelling in the Father. These are the same words used to describe unity dwelling or being one with the Father. Hence, this further supports the position that when Jesus spoke of mansions or dwelling in the Father's house, this is what He was referring to. The subject of His death is a recurring theme throughout the passage context. However, this was the avenue through which He would prepare a place for humanity in the Father's house or restore us to the family of God.

By considering the entire passage context, we are furnished with a better understanding of what Jesus was conveying in John Chapter 14 as opposed to a fragmented perspective. Instead of the idea of a building, the concept of mansions pertains to the following:

- Becoming sons of God and being one with the Father and members of His family.
- Abiding in Christ and manifesting righteous character.
- Being one with the Father results in persecution.

CHAPTER SIX

Eternal Inheritance

N ow that we have a proper perspective of the Father's
house, along with clarity concerning mansions, it is
only fitting that we address the subject of where believers
will spend eternity. Certainly, if the notion of a "home in
the sky" is not supported by Scripture, then what does it say
regarding our eternal inheritance? Once again, the answer
to this question can be found in the book of Genesis as it is
connected to God's original purpose for humanity. In essence,
the book of Genesis is not just an account of creation or a
compilation of stories. It serves as the blueprint for God's
purpose for humanity.

According to Genesis, God's intent was for humanity to
dwell on Earth and have dominion over creation.

> 26. And God said, Let us make man in our image,
> after our likeness: and let them have dominion
> over the fish of the sea, and over the fowl of the
> air, and over the cattle, and over all the earth, and

over every creeping thing that creepeth upon the
earth.

27. So God created man in his own image, in the
image of God created he him; male and female
created he them.

28. And God blessed them, and God said unto them,
Be fruitful, and multiply, and replenish the earth,
and subdue it: and have dominion over the fish of
the sea, and over the fowl of the air, and over every
living thing that moveth upon the earth. (Genesis
1:26-28)

The word "dominion" means the following:

- Control
- The power to govern
- Sovereignty
- A territory or sphere of influence or control; a
realm
- The territory subject to the control of a government

Based on Genesis 1:26, humanity was given the earth
as a territory of influence or a realm to exercise dominion
over. Simply put, mankind was given government control of
the earth. Furthermore, with the word "dominion" having
kingdom significance, this means humanity operated within a
kingdom environment. God set up His kingdom/government
on Earth and gave His son Adam (Luke 3:38) government
responsibility for it. Based on this premise, Earth became a
colony of the kingdom of heaven as God wanted to influence

Earth with the culture of heaven. However, as a result of teachings like "mansions in heaven," the church has created an appetite for going to heaven, whereas God is more concerned with bringing heaven to Earth. If it was the Lord's perpetual intent to have humanity in heaven, He would have placed us there from the beginning. In principle, God does not want to colonize heaven with Earth but rather, colonize Earth with the influence of heaven.

The Earth and dominion over it were given to humanity as an inheritance. However, through disobedience, man forfeited his governing influence or dominion over the earth and delivered it to Satan. Just to be clear, Psalm 24:1 indicates the earth is the Lord's and the fullness thereof, and that has not changed. Nevertheless, what Satan possesses is government control of the earth, which is manifested through the power or kingdom of darkness (Colossians 1:13). Hence, the details of the account of the Devil tempting Jesus in Luke 4:5-7:

5. And the devil, taking him up into an high mountain, *shewed unto him all the kingdoms of the world in a moment of time.*

6. And the devil said unto him, *All this power will I give thee, and the glory of them: for that is delivered unto me; and to whomsoever I will I give it.*

7. If thou therefore wilt worship me, all shall be thine.

What the Devil was offering Jesus was dominion or government control over the earth. Notice that he showed Him the kingdoms or dominions of the world and the glory of them (Matthew 4:8). He was simply offering Him what Adam had originally possessed. Consequently, throughout Scripture, the Lord's objective was to restore the inheritance that was relinquished. However, this time, He would make it eternal in nature so that it would never be lost again. Through Christ, the sons of God have the promise of eternal inheritance (Hebrews 9:15).

GOD'S PROMISE TO ABRAHAM

In Genesis 12:1-3, the Lord promised Abraham that in him all nations shall be blessed. Essentially, this blessing was the promise of eternal redemption and eternal inheritance through Christ (Hebrews 9:11-15). Throughout Scripture, this is simply referred to as "the promise."

13. For when God made promise to Abraham, because he could swear by no greater, he sware by himself,
14. Saying, Surely blessing I will bless thee, and multiplying I will multiply thee (Hebrews 6:13-14).

That the blessing of Abraham might come on the Gentiles through Jesus Christ; that we might receive the promise of the Spirit through faith. (Galatians 3:14)

Galatians 3:8 says that when God made the promise to Abraham, He was in effect preaching the gospel to him.

Contained in the promise was the entirety of the gospel message, which is eternal redemption and eternal inheritance.

What is interesting is that based on the scriptural relationship between Hebrews 6:13-14 and Galatians 3:14, we have a precise understanding of how the promise was going to be fulfilled. Galatians 3:14 says very plainly that "the blessing" or "the promise" of Abraham is obtained when we receive the Holy Spirit. Therefore, when we receive the Holy Spirit or the Spirit of adoption (which makes us members of the Father's house), we simultaneously receive the promise of eternal redemption and eternal inheritance.

Moreover, as we have discussed, when we receive the Holy Spirit, the Father makes His abode with us. Simultaneously, we also make our abode with Him and become one with Him. Therefore, as these are also components of God's promise to Abraham, it is comprehensive because it allows us to be adopted into the Father's house as sons.

As a point of reference, Galatians 3:16 indicates that "the promise" was made to both Abraham and his seed, meaning Christ. Therefore, Jesus was the one destined to fulfill the promise of eternal redemption and eternal inheritance. This is why Galatians 3:29 says, "And if ye be Christ's, then are ye Abraham's seed, and heirs according to the promise."

Kingdom dominion or inheritance was lost through sin. However, before it could be restored, there first had to be redemption. Redemption is therefore a prerequisite to inheritance. However, for an eternal inheritance to exist, the redemption had to be of the same nature; therefore, unlike what the law provided, redemption had to be eternal (Hebrews 9:11-15). As a principle, redemption and inheritance are interrelated as there can be no kingdom dominion without redemption.

In light of God's original purpose and with the mandate of kingdom restoration, Jesus Christ's first announcement in Matthew 4:17 was, "Repent: for the kingdom of heaven is at hand." Notice even in this pronouncement that there was a combination of redemption and kingdom dominion (inheritance). In fact, the message of the kingdom was the only message Jesus taught. Let's look at the two components of the promise God made to Abraham.

ETERNAL REDEMPTION

Recall that the word "redeem" means to buy back or to ransom. It involves the payment of a price to recover from the power of another. After Adam sinned, humanity became subjects of the kingdom or jurisdiction of darkness (Colossians 1:13). Additionally, because there is always an association between kingdom and family, this was also our family affiliation. Therefore, to reconcile humanity to the kingdom of God and His family, a ransom had to be paid. However, this payment was based on the premise established in Hebrews 9:22, which states that without the shedding of blood there is no remission or forgiveness. Accordingly, 1 Peter 1:18-19 says that we were not redeemed with corruptible things such as gold or silver but with the precious blood of Christ.

Under the law, redemption was temporal as opposed to eternal. Hence, Hebrews 10:1 says that the law was only a shadow of good things to come (Hebrews 10:1). Therefore, the sacrifices were offered every year because it was impossible for the blood of bulls and goats to take away sins (Hebrews 10:3-4). However, Jesus came in the form of a man, thus, fulfilling the law of a kinsman redeemer and offered Himself as a sacrifice for sin. Unlike the sacrifices of the law, Hebrews 10:12 says that after *one* sacrifice for sins, He forever sat down at the right hand of God. This is an indication that as it pertains to sacrifice for sin, redemption is a completed work, and Christ has secured eternal redemption for us.

11. But Christ being come an high priest of good things to come, by a greater and more perfect tabernacle, not made with hands, that is to say, not of this building;
12. Neither by the blood of goats and calves, but by his own blood he entered in once into the holy place, *having obtained eternal redemption for us.* (Hebrews 9:11-12)

As a point of reference, eternal doesn't just mean that which is everlasting, but it also means immutable or unchangeable. Additionally, the term eternal redemption is distinctly used to contrast the temporal redemption that was offered under the law. Hebrews 10:9-10 says that as a result of the new covenant, those who believe in Christ are sanctified through the sacrifice of Christ, which He offered once and for all. Not only was the sacrifice once and for all but also its impact.

Moreover, Acts 3:25-26 emphasizes the fact that redemption was a component of the promise God made to Abraham.

25. Ye are the children of the prophets, and of *the covenant which God made with our fathers, saying unto Abraham, And in thy seed shall all the kindreds of the earth be blessed.*
26. Unto you first God, having raised up his Son Jesus, sent him *to bless you, in turning away every one of you from his iniquities.* (Acts 3:25-26)

The above passage, in defining redemption, uses the phrase "turning away everyone from their iniquities." This speaks of deliverance from the allegiance or dominion of sin.

ETERNAL INHERITANCE

As mentioned at the beginning of this chapter, there is a corresponding relationship between redemption and kingdom dominion or our inheritance. Therefore, to completely restore what Adam lost as a result of transgression, the second component in the promise to Abraham involved restored kingdom dominion.

> For the promise, that he should be the heir of the world, was not to Abraham, or to his seed, through the law, but through the righteousness of faith. (Romans 4:13)

With the promise to Abraham involving both eternal redemption and eternal inheritance, the former paved the way for the latter. Hence, without redemption, there can be no inheritance. Based on Romans 4:13, the promise to Abraham that he would be the heir or inheritor of the world is a promise of restored kingdom dominion and government. This is obviously connected to God's original purpose for humanity. The word "world" in the passage is the Greek word *kosmos*. It encompasses all that pertains to the earth including government and territory. The word "world" means the following:

- A proper and harmonious arrangement or constitution
- Order
- Government
- The earth
- The universe
- The inhabitants of the earth
- World affairs
- The aggregate of things pertaining to the earth
- The whole circle of earthly goods, endowments, riches, advantages, pleasures, etc.

In simple terms, inheritance is what is given to someone as a possession. However, as it pertains to Scripture, inheritance is explicitly reserved for sons, which again, is not gender-specific. From the beginning, humanity's inheritance in the capacity of sons, was the earth and dominion over it (Genesis 1:26). Therefore, contained within the promise that God made to Abraham is the restoration of kingdom dominion resembling the conditions that existed under the first Adam. It is a promise of dominion over all the earth. Redemption equals sonship and sonship results in inheritance. However, to ensure that the inheritance would not be lost again, the Lord not only provided eternal redemption but also eternal inheritance.

> And for this cause he is the mediator of the new testament, that by means of death, for the redemption of the transgressions that were under the first testament, *they which are called might receive the promise of eternal inheritance.* (Hebrews 9:15)

As the promise of restored kingdom dominion was made to both Abraham and Christ, this time, the government will be established under the last Adam (Jesus Christ), the only begotten Son of the Father.

6. For unto us a child is born, unto us a son is given: and *the government shall be upon his shoulder*: and his name shall be called Wonderful, Counseller, The mighty God, The everlasting Father, The Prince of Peace.

7. *Of the increase of his government and peace there shall be no end,* upon the throne of David, and upon his kingdom, to order it, and to establish it with judgment and with justice from henceforth

even forever. The zeal of the LORD of hosts will perform this. (Isaiah 9:6-7)

Even while teaching His disciples to pray, notice specifically the words of Jesus in Matthew Chapter 6. He says, "Our Father which art in heaven, Hallowed be thy name. Thy kingdom come. Thy will be done in earth, as it is in heaven." Hence, Christ will establish His kingdom on the earth, and as sons and fellow heirs, we will reign with Him (on Earth). This further negates the notion of mansions in heaven as that is not where the sons of God will spend eternity.

Blessed and holy is he that hath part in the first resurrection: on such the second death hath no power, but they shall be priests of God and of Christ, and shall reign with him a thousand years. (Revelation 20:4)

When we take into account God's original purpose for humanity and the mandate of dominion over the earth, it becomes abundantly clear that His purpose has not changed. Furthermore, when we search the Scriptures, there is conclusive evidence that the earth and dominion over it have been provided as an inheritance for the sons of God.

Blessed are the meek: for they shall inherit the earth. (Matthew 5:5)

The heaven, even the heavens, are the LORD'S: but the earth hath he given to the children of men. (Psalm 115:16)

Furthermore, in the promise that God made to Abraham (and Christ), the land was given as an everlasting possession.

7. And I will establish my covenant between me and thee and thy seed after thee in their generations for an everlasting covenant, to be a God unto thee, and to thy seed after thee.

8. And I will give unto thee, and to thy seed after thee, the land wherein thou art a stranger, all the land of Canaan, for an everlasting possession; and I will be their God. (Genesis 17:7-8)

9. And they sung a new song, saying, Thou art worthy to take the book, and to open the seals thereof: for thou wast slain, and hast redeemed us to God by thy blood out of every kindred, and tongue, and people, and nation;

10. And hast made us unto our God kings and priests: *and we shall reign on the earth.* (Revelation 5:9-10)

Additionally, Hebrews 12:28 in acknowledgment that we will receive a kingdom, which cannot be moved admonishes believers to have grace, whereby we may serve God acceptably with reverence and godly fear.

Christ's sacrifice makes it possible for humanity to be adopted into the Father's house by the Spirit of God or the Spirit of adoption. This signifies eternal redemption. Hence, those who believe in Him are also made sons of God. By becoming sons of the Father's house, we are made heirs and joint heirs with Christ. This speaks of eternal inheritance. Again, Romans 8:15-17 provides the best summary for this conclusion.

15. For ye have not received the spirit of bondage again to fear; but ye have received the Spirit of adoption, whereby we cry, Abba, Father.
16. The Spirit itself beareth witness with our spirit, that we are the children of God:
17. And if children, then heirs; heirs of God, and joint-heirs with Christ; if so be that we suffer with him, that we may be also glorified together. (Romans 8:15-17)

GOD'S KINGDOM ON EARTH

In Daniel Chapter 2, King Nebuchadnezzar had a dream in which he saw a statue. It had a head of fine gold, breast, and arms of silver, belly, and thighs of brass, legs of iron with feet consisting of part iron and part clay (Daniel 2:31-33). Furthermore, in the dream, he saw a stone cut out of the mountain without hands. It shattered the image. In addition, Daniel 2:34-35 says that the stone became a great mountain and filled the whole earth. Based on the dream, the Lord revealed to Daniel that the statue represented four kingdoms that would exercise dominion over the earth for a period of time. The stone cut out of the mountain "without hands" represents that which is heavenly and points to the kingdom of God. The dream pertained to kingdom rule of the earth over the ages culminating with the establishment of the kingdom of God on Earth. This will be the final kingdom on Earth that will consume all the other kingdoms. It will be headed by Jesus Christ.

> 44. And in the days of these kings shall the God of heaven set up a kingdom, which shall never be destroyed: and the kingdom shall not be left to other people, but it shall break in pieces and consume all these kingdoms, and it shall stand for ever.
>
> 45. Forasmuch as thou sawest that the stone was cut out of the mountain without hands, and that it brake in pieces the iron, the brass, the clay, the silver, and the gold; the great God hath made known to the king what shall come to pass hereafter: and the dream is certain, and the interpretation thereof sure. (Daniel 2:44-45)

At its core, the Bible is fundamentally an account of the establishment of the kingdom of God on Earth. This was evident from the beginning and throughout the ages, this purpose has not changed. To this end, Scripture offers abundant proof concerning the establishment of the kingdom of God on Earth.

> 3. Then shall the LORD go forth, and fight against those nations, as when he fought in the day of battle.
>
> 4. And his feet shall stand in that day upon the mount of Olives, which is before Jerusalem on the east, and the mount of Olives shall cleave in the

midst thereof toward the east and toward the west, and there shall be a very great valley; and half of the mountain shall remove toward the north, and half of it toward the south. (Zechariah 14:3-4)

9. And the LORD shall be king over all the earth: in that day shall there be one LORD, and his name one. (Zechariah 14:9)

1. And I saw a new heaven and a new earth: for the first heaven and the first earth were passed away; and there was no more sea.

2. And I John saw the holy city, new Jerusalem, coming down from God out of heaven, prepared as a bride adorned for her husband.

3. And I heard a great voice out of heaven saying, Behold, the tabernacle of God is with men, and he will dwell with them, and they shall be his people, and God himself shall be with them, and be their God. (Revelation 21:1-3)

STRANGERS AND PILGRIMS

The concept of mansions in heaven is further fueled by the notion of being strangers and pilgrims on the earth. While this characterization attributed to believers is true, it certainly needs qualification. Generally speaking, a stranger and pilgrim is someone who travels from his/her home country and journeys in foreign lands. Based on this premise, many believers regard heaven as their home country and the foreign place is Earth. Hence, there is an intense desire to return home, especially with the notion that mansions are there.

For the sons of God, we are indeed strangers and pilgrims on Earth. However, this reality does not constitute heaven as our home. In truth, this is really a discussion of citizenship. In this vein, Philippians 3:20 says, "For our conversation is in heaven; from whence also we look for the Saviour, the Lord Jesus Christ."

The word "conversation" in the passage is the Greek word *politeuma,* which means the administration of a commonwealth or a commonwealth of citizens. Hence, this passage refers to citizenship in the kingdom of God. Therefore, as believers, despite residing on Earth, this is not the basis of our citizenship. Our citizenship is associated with the kingdom of God, for we are strangers on the earth.

In all, the Bible speaks of two distinct kingdoms, one is the kingdom of God and the other being the kingdom of darkness (Colossians 1:13). Additionally, citizenship and family affinity are directly associated with each kingdom. As a result of Adam's transgression, humanity became estranged from the kingdom of God. Furthermore, we became citizens of the kingdom of darkness and that was also our family affinity. However, through Christ, those who believe in Him become citizens of the kingdom of God and members of His family. Therefore, regardless of being on Earth, our citizenship is heavenly. For example, based on natural birth, I was born in the Bahamas and consequently, I am a Bahamian citizen. However, by spiritual birth, the true essence of who I am is a citizen of the kingdom of heaven. Hence, my spiritual birth made me a stranger on Earth.

As a foundation, Hebrews Chapter 11 provides the account of those in the Old Testament who as a result of embracing the promises of God confessed that they were strangers and pilgrims on the earth.

13. These all died in faith, not having received the promises, but having seen them afar off, and were persuaded of them, and embraced them, and confessed that they were strangers and pilgrims on the earth.
14. For they that say such things declare plainly that they seek a country.
15. And truly, if they had been mindful of that country from whence they came out, they might have had opportunity to have returned.
16. But now they desire a better country, that is, an heavenly: wherefore God is not ashamed to be called their God: for he hath prepared for them a city. (Hebrews 11:13-16)

Recall that the promises God made to Abraham included eternal redemption and eternal inheritance. Particularly, with eternal inheritance being associated with the kingdom of God, this caused them to desire a better country, one that is heavenly as opposed to one that is earthly. In fact, to qualify this, Hebrews 11:9 says that Abraham looked for a city, which hath foundations whose builder and maker is God. In this regard, Hebrews 11:16 says that God has prepared for them a city. Therefore, because they saw themselves belonging to a heavenly city or having a heavenly citizenship, they regarded themselves as strangers and pilgrims on Earth.

The concept of citizenship is nothing new but dates back to ancient Greece and Rome. The word "citizenship" comes from the Latin words for city, which are *urbs* and *civitas*. The first one pertains to the actual physical city, while the second points to the community aspect of the city. The word "city" is associated with citizenship because, in the earlier days of human governments, people identified themselves as belonging to cities more than countries. Hence, government and citizenship were associated with the city. The progression of citizenship in relation to a country came later. What does it mean to be a citizen? The word "citizen" as defined by *Merriam-Webster's Dictionary* means:

- A person who legally belongs to a country and has the rights and protection of that country
- A native or naturalized person who owes allegiance to a government and is entitled to protection from it

Furthermore, every kingdom or country has principles that govern the lives of its citizens and is often referred to as the constitution. Therefore, when Jesus came and announced that the kingdom of heaven was at hand, the first thing He did was teach on the principles or the constitution of the kingdom of God. Additionally, being a stranger and pilgrim on Earth also carries with it the responsibility of not conforming to the principles or dictates of this world. Hence, 1 Peter 2:11 says, "Dearly beloved, I beseech you as strangers and pilgrims, abstain from fleshly lusts, which war against the soul."

In summary, the characterization of being strangers and pilgrims on the earth has nothing to do with heaven being the home of believers but rather being citizens of the kingdom of God.

THE GIFT OF GOD IS EVERLASTING LIFE

To be clear, the Bible never said that the gift of God is heaven. It specifically says that the gift of God is everlasting life. John 3:16 says, "For God so love the world, that he gave his only begotten Son and whosoever believeth in him should not perish but have everlasting life." The word "everlasting" is synonymous with eternal. On that note, eternal life doesn't start when we die. It starts from the moment we are born again. Because the Spirit of God dwells in those who believe in Jesus, we presently have the gift of eternal life. To support this, both John 3:36 and John 6:47 point out that whoever believes in the Son of God already has eternal life. Moreover, John 5:24 says, "Verily, verily, I say unto you, He that heareth my word, and believeth in Him that sent me, hath everlasting life, and shall not come into condemnation; but is passed from death into life."

Additionally, eternal life doesn't just refer to unending years, but it also pertains to the quality of life. For what is the purpose of having the life of God if it does not enhance your existence? Throughout Scripture, there is always a correlation between light and life (Genesis Chapter 1; John 1:4, John 8:12). Light always causes life to be created or manifested and vice versa. Hence, when we receive the life of the Father, along with it also comes light. In Scripture, light speaks of wisdom, righteous character, life, truth, etc. On the other hand, darkness, which is the antithesis of light, figuratively speaks of ignorance, blindness, sorrow, despair, hatred, death, etc. Moreover, Ephesians 5:8 categorizes the sons of God as children of light while James 1:7 references God as the Father of lights.

As a result of the gift of Christ, Romans 5:17 says believers shall reign in life through Jesus Christ. The word "reign" means to exercise the highest influence or to exercise kingly power. Again, this is not when we die but in this present life. This further supports the premise that eternal life is not limited to quantity but also includes our quality of life.

To support the position of this book, the focus of this chapter is on having a comprehensive discussion regarding the eternal inheritance of believers. From the beginning, God's purpose has always been to provide the earth as an inheritance for His sons, which includes dominion or government control over it. When the Lord returns to set up His kingdom on Earth, as joint heirs, believers shall rule and reign with Him on Earth for all eternity. Why limit your thinking to a house or a "so-called" mansion when it is the Father's intent or good pleasure to give us an entire kingdom and dominion over the whole Earth? Based on the words of popular songs such as, "I'm tryin' to make heaven my home," the church has a longing desire to go to heaven. However, as said before, God's purpose has always been to bring the influence of heaven to Earth.

CONCLUSION

Some time ago, while teaching a class on rightly dividing the Word of God, I mentioned to the students that the church had an incorrect perspective regarding mansions in heaven. Obviously, there was some resistance to what I said because it went against the traditional teaching of the church. Even though I had not fully developed the subject at the time, I was convinced based on Scripture and inspiration from the Holy Spirit that the concept of mansions in heaven has been misrepresented.

In the years that followed, by means of study, the Lord revealed to me the truth in reference to mansions and that it pertained to be being members of the Father's house or His family.

The subtitle of this book, "It's a Family Affair," reveals the true intent of Jesus' message. As opposed to the notion of a house or building, the purpose of the Father was always to have a family, particularly a family of sons. This was evident from the book of Genesis. Therefore, in John 14:2, when Jesus refers to mansions in the Father's house, He's really speaking of a family concept. He is expressing the relationship between the Father and His sons where He dwells in us, and we dwell in Him. As a Son representing His Father's house,

Jesus was tasked with introducing humanity to God as Father and incorporating us into the family of God.

The product of truth is liberty. Through studying and writing this book, I felt a sense of freedom and an appreciation for the Father's purpose. As opposed to the traditional concept, it is actually a message of reconciliation, restoration, and unity with the Father. It speaks resoundingly of being one with the Father and us being one with Him.

The Scripture makes it abundantly clear in John 3:16 that the gift of God is eternal life, and this is wonderful. However, it is also clear that eternal life will be enjoyed on Earth in accordance with God's original purpose from the beginning. It will not be in heaven. As we have discovered throughout this book, God's purpose has not changed, and Scripture is consistent in conveying this message.

This book is truly a product of much prayer, study, and inspiration from the Father. It reveals His heart toward us, His purpose to have a family of sons, and the true inheritance He has predetermined for us.

REFERENCES

- AMG Publishers, The Hebrew-Greek Key Study Bible. Editor, Zodhiates, S. © 1995.
- Stanphil, Ira © 1949 Mansion over the Hilltop.
- Time [Def.] Strong's Concordance with Hebrew and Greek Lexicon Retrieved January 10, 2018 from https://www.blueletterbible.org/lang/Lexicon/Lexicon.cfm?strongs=G2540&t=KJV
- World [Def.] Strong's Concordance with Hebrew and Greek Lexicon Retrieved January 13, 2018 from https://www.blueletterbible.org/lang/Lexicon/Lexicon.cfm?strongs=G165&t=KJV
- Malmin, Ken and Kevin J. Conner, © 1983, Context of Scripture, A Textbook on How to Interpret the Bible Interpreting the Scriptures.
- Butler, Clement C, ©2017 God's Eternal Purpose Volume 1: The Establishment of God's Kingdom.
- Butler, Clement C, ©2017 God's Eternal Purpose Volume 2: The Identity of the sons of God: The Image of Jesus Christ.
- Cleare, Dr. Betty, © 1994 Rightly Dividing the Word, Perspective of Scripture, New Life Christian Centre.
- Butler, Clement C, © 2015 The Volume of the Book: Insights into Rightly Dividing the Word of Truth.

- Strong, James © 2009 Strong's Exhaustive Concordance of the Bible.
- Context [Def] Retrieved January 15, 2018 from https://literarydevices.net/context/
- Get to the Point, Toastmasters Competent Communicator Manual, Toastmasters International
- Only Begotten [Def.] Strong's Concordance with Hebrew and Greek Lexicon Retrieved January 18, 2018 from https://www.blueletterbible.org/lang/Lexicon/Lexicon.cfm?strongs=G3439&t=KJV
- Bosom [Def.] Strong's Concordance with Hebrew and Greek Lexicon Retrieved January 25, 2020 from https://www.blueletterbible.org/lang/Lexicon/Lexicon.cfm?strongs=G2859&t=KJV
- Father [Def.] Strong's Concordance with Hebrew and Greek Lexicon Retrieved February 1, 2018 from https://www.blueletterbible.org/lang/Lexicon/Lexicon.cfm?strongs=G3962&t=KJV
- Declared [Def.] Strong's Concordance with Hebrew and Greek Lexicon Retrieved February 5, 2018 from https://www.blueletterbible.org/lang/Lexicon/Lexicon.cfm?strongs=G1834&t=KJV
- House [Def.] Strong's Concordance with Hebrew and Greek Lexicon Retrieved February 8, 2018 from https://www.blueletterbible.org/lang/Lexicon/Lexicon.cfm?strongs=G3614&t=KJV
- Adoption [Def.] Strong's Concordance with Hebrew and Greek Lexicon Retrieved February 15, 2018 from https://www.blueletterbible.org/lang/Lexicon/Lexicon.cfm?strongs=G5206&t=KJV

- Mansions [Def.] Strong's Concordance with Hebrew and Greek Lexicon Retrieved February 20, 2018 from https://www.blueletterbible.org/lang/Lexicon/Lexicon.cfm?strongs=G3438&t=KJV
- Abode [Def.] Strong's Concordance with Hebrew and Greek Lexicon Retrieved February 22, 2018 from https://www.blueletterbible.org/lang/Lexicon/Lexicon.cfm?strongs=G3438&t=KJV
- Redeem [Def.] Strong's Concordance with Hebrew and Greek Lexicon Retrieved February 23, 2018 from https://www.blueletterbible.org/lang/Lexicon/Lexicon.cfm?strongs=G1805&t=KJV
- Atonement [Def.] Strong's Concordance with Hebrew and Greek Lexicon Retrieved February 25, 2018 from https://www.blueletterbible.org/lang/Lexicon/Lexicon.cfm?strongs=G2643&t=KJV
- Dominion [Def.]. Free Dictionary by Farlex Online. In the Free Dictionary by Farlex Retrieved February 28, 2016, from http://www.thefreedictionary.com/dominion
- Children [Def.] Strong's Concordance with Hebrew and Greek Lexicon Retrieved February 28, 2018 from https://www.blueletterbible.org/lang/Lexicon/Lexicon.cfm?strongs=G5043&t=KJV
- World [Def.] Strong's Concordance with Hebrew and Greek Lexicon Retrieved March 1 2018 from https://www.blueletterbible.org/lang/Lexicon/Lexicon.cfm?strongs=G2889&t=KJV
- Pilgrim [Def.] Strong's Concordance with Hebrew and Greek Lexicon Retrieved September 4, 2020 from

https://www.blueletterbible.org/lang/Lexicon/Lexicon.cfm?strongs=G3927&t=KJV

- Conversation [Def.] Strong's Concordance with Hebrew and Greek Lexicon Retrieved September 7, 2020 from https://www.blueletterbible.org/lang/Lexicon/Lexicon.cfm?strongs=G4175&t=KJV
- Citizenship [Def.] Merriam-Webster Online. Retrieved September 8, 2020, from http://www.merriam-webster.com/dictionary/citizenship
- Citizenship [Def.] Vocabulary.com Online. Retrieved September 8, 2020 from www.vocabulary.com/dictionary/citizenship
- Booth, Dawn, photographer, "Armor of God" [Contenders for the Faith]. Photograph. 2010. Retrieved December 9, 2020 from https://www.google.com/search?rlz=1C1CHBF_enBS731BS752&source=univ&tbm=isch&q=dawn+booth+photo+of+the+whole+armor+of+God&sa=X&ved=2ahUKEwi7yvq-gsTtAhX-kAp0JHVPXCNUQjJkEegQIBRAB&biw=1536&bih=755#imgrc=jul37HAxzbtFjM